Divine Healing

Divine Healing

A Series of Addresses and a Personal Testimony

By the REV. ANDREW MURRAY

CHRISTIAN LITERATURE CRUSADE
Fort Washington, Pennsylvania 19034

CHRISTIAN LITERATURE CRUSADE

U.S.A.
Box 1449, Fort Washington, PA 19034

GREAT BRITAIN
51 The Dean, Alresford, Hants., SO24 9BJ

AUSTRALIA
P.O. Box 91, Pennant Hills, N.S.W. 2120

NEW ZEALAND
P.O. Box 1203, Palmerston North

First published 1934 by the Victory Press
London, England, S.W.4.

This printing 1993
ISBN 0-87508-375-7

Scriptures are quoted from the King James Version
of the Bible unless otherwise identified:
ASV = American Standard Version
RSV = Revised Standard Version
RV = English Revised Version

PRINTED IN THE UNITED STATES OF AMERICA

CONTENTS

v

PREFACE

The publication of this work may be regarded as a testimony of my faith in divine healing. After being stopped for more than two years in the exercise of my ministry, I was healed by the mercy of God in answer to the prayer of those who see in Him "the Lord that healeth thee" (Exod. 15:26).

This healing, granted to faith, has been the source of rich spiritual blessing to me. I have clearly seen that the Church possesses in Jesus, our Divine Healer, an inestimable treasure, which she does not yet know how to appreciate. I have been convinced anew of that which the Word of God teaches us in this matter, and of what the Lord expects of us; and I am sure that if Christians learned to realize practically the presence of the Lord that healeth, their spiritual life would thereby be developed and sanctified. I can therefore no longer keep silence, and I publish here a series of meditations, with the view of showing, according to the Word of God, that "the prayer of faith" (James 5:15) is the means appointed by God for the cure of the sick, that this truth is in perfect accord with Holy Scripture, and that the study of this truth is essential for every one who would see the Lord manifest His power and His glory in the midst of His children.

Chapter 1

PARDON AND HEALING

But that ye may know that the Son of man hath power on earth to forgive sins (then saith he to the sick of the palsy), Arise, take up thy bed and go unto thine house. (Matt. 9:6)

In man two natures are combined. He is at the same time spirit and matter, heaven and earth, soul and body. For this reason, on one side he is the son of God, and on the other he is doomed to destruction because of the Fall; sin in his soul and sickness in his body bear witness to the right which death has over him. It is the twofold nature which has been redeemed by divine grace. When the Psalmist calls upon all that is within him to bless the Lord for His benefits, he cries, "Bless the Lord, O my soul, . . . who forgiveth all thine iniquities, who healeth all thy diseases" (Ps. 103:2-3). When Isaiah foretells the deliverance of his people, he adds, "The inhabitant

1

shall not say, I am sick; the people that dwell therein shall be forgiven their iniquity" (Isa. 33:24).

This prediction was accomplished beyond all anticipation when Jesus the Redeemer came down to this earth. How numerous were the healings wrought by Him who was come to establish upon earth the kingdom of heaven! By His own acts and afterward by the commands which He left for His disciples, He showed us clearly that the preaching of the Gospel and the healing of the sick went together in the salvation which He came to bring. Both are given as evident proof of His mission as the Messiah: "The blind receive their sight, and the lame walk . . . and the poor have the gospel preached to them" (Matt. 11:5). Jesus, who took upon Himself the soul and body of man, delivers both in equal measure from the consequences of sin.

This truth is nowhere more evident or better demonstrated than in the history of the paralytic. The Lord Jesus begins by saying to him, "Thy sins be forgiven thee," after which He adds, "Arise, take up thy bed, and go." The pardon of sin and the healing of sickness complete one another, for in the eyes of God, who sees our entire nature, sin and sickness are as closely united as the body and the soul.

With us, sin belongs to the spiritual domain; we recognize that it is under God's just displeasure, justly condemned by Him, while sickness, on the contrary, seems only a part of the present condition of our nature, having nothing to do with God's condemnation and His righteousness. Some go so far as to say that sickness is a proof of the love and grace of God.

But neither the Scripture nor Jesus Christ Himself ever speak of sickness in this light, nor do they ever present sickness as a blessing, as a proof of God's love which should be borne with patience. The Lord spoke to the disciples of divers sufferings which they should have to bear, but when He speaks of sickness, it is always as of an evil caused by sin and Satan, and from which we should be delivered. Very solemnly He declared that every disciple of His would have to bear his cross (Matt. 16:24), but He never taught one sick person to resign himself to be sick. Everywhere, Jesus healed the sick; everywhere, He dealt with healing as one of the graces belonging to the kingdom of heaven. Sin in the soul and sickness in the body both bear witness to the power of Satan, and "the Son of God was manifested that he might destroy the works of the devil" (I John 3:8).

Jesus came to deliver men from sin and sickness that He might make known the love of the Father. In His actions, in His teaching of the disciples, in the work of the apostles, pardon and healing are always found together. Either the one or the other may doubtless appear more in relief, according to the development, or the faith, of those to whom they spoke. Sometimes it was healing which prepared the way for the acceptance of forgiveness; sometimes it was forgiveness which preceded the healing, which, coming afterward, became a seal to it. In the early part of His ministry, Jesus cured many of the sick, finding them ready to believe in the possibility of their healing. In this way, He sought to influence hearts to receive Himself as Him who is able to pardon sin. When He saw that the paralytic could receive pardon at once, He began with that which was of the greatest importance, after which came the healing which put a seal on the pardon which had been accorded to him.

We see, by the accounts given in the Gospels, that it was more difficult for the Jews at that time to believe in the pardon of their sins than in divine healing. Now, it is just the contrary. The Christian Church has heard so much of the preaching of the forgiveness of sins that the thirsty soul easily receives this message of grace; but it is not the same with divine healing. That is rarely spoken of; the believers who have experienced it are not many. It is true that healing is not given in this day as in those times, to the multitudes whom Christ healed without any previous conversion. In order to receive healing, it is necessary to begin by confession of sin and the purpose to live a holy life. This is without doubt the reason why people find it more difficult to believe in healing than in forgiveness; and this is also why those who receive healing receive at the same time new spiritual blessing, feel more closely united to the Lord Jesus, and learn to love and serve Him better. Unbelief may attempt to separate these two gifts, but they are always united in Christ. He is always the same Savior both of the soul and ·of the body, equally ready to grant pardon and healing. The redeemed may always cry, "Bless the Lord, O my soul . . . who forgiveth all thine iniquities, who healeth all thy diseases" (Ps. 103:2-3).

Chapter 2

BECAUSE OF YOUR UNBELIEF

Then came the disciples to Jesus apart, and said, Why could not we cast him out?

And Jesus said unto them, Because of your unbelief: for verily I say unto you, If ye have faith as a grain of mustard seed, ye shall say unto this mountain, Remove hence to yonder place; and it shall remove; and nothing shall be impossible to you. (Matt. 17:19-20)

When the Lord Jesus sent His disciples into different parts of Palestine, He endued them with a double power, to cast out unclean spirits and to heal all sickness and all infirmity (Matt. 10:1). He did the same for the seventy who came back to Him with joy, saying, "Lord, even the spirits are subject unto us through Thy name" (Luke 10:17 RV). On the day of the Transfiguration, while the Lord was still upon the mountain, a father brought his son who was possessed with a demon, to His disciples, beseeching them to cast out the evil spirit, but they could not. After Jesus had cured the child, the disciples asked Him why they had been unable to do it themselves as in other cases. He answered them, "Because of your unbelief." It was, then, their unbelief, and not the will of God which had been the cause of their defeat.

In our days, divine healing is very little believed in, because it has almost entirely disappeared from the Christian Church. One may ask the reason, and here are the two answers which have been given. The greater number think that miracles, the gift of healing included, should be limited to the time of the primitive Church, that their object was to establish the first foundation of Christianity, but that from that time, circumstances have altered. Other believers say unhesitatingly that if the Church has lost these gifts, it is by her own fault. It is because she has become worldly that the Spirit acts but feebly in her. It is because she has not remained in direct and habitual relation with the full power of the unseen world. But if she were to see anew springing up within her men and women who live the life of faith and of the Holy Spirit, entirely consecrated to their God, she would see again the manifestation of the same gifts as in former times.

Which of these two opinions coincides with

the Word of God? Is it by the will of God that the "gifts of healing" have been suppressed, or is it rather man who is responsible for it? Is it the will of God that miracles should not take place? Will He in consequence of this no longer give the faith which produces them? Or again, is it the Church which has been guilty of lacking faith?

What Does the Scripture Say?

The Bible does not authorize us, either by the words of the Lord or His apostles, to believe that the gifts of healing were granted only to the early times of the Church; on the contrary, the promise which Jesus made to the apostles when He gave them instructions concerning their mission, shortly before His ascension, appear to us applicable to all times (Mark 16:15-18). Paul places the gift of healing among the operations of the Holy Spirit. James gives a precise command on this matter without any restriction of time. The entire Scriptures declare that these graces will be granted according to the measure of the Spirit and of faith.

It is also alleged that at the outset of each new dispensation God works miracles, that it is His ordinary course of action; but it is nothing of the kind. Think of the people of God in the former dispensation, in the time of Abraham, all through the life of Moses, in the exodus from Egypt, under Joshua, in the time of the Judges and of Samuel, under the reign of David and other godly kings up to Daniel's time. During more than a thousand years, miracles took place.

But, it is said, miracles were much more necessary in the early days of Christianity than later. But what about the power of heathenism even in this day, wherever the Gospel seeks to combat it? It is impossible to admit that miracles should have been more needful for the heathen in Ephesus (Acts 19:11-12) than for the heathen of Africa in the present day. And if we think of the ignorance and unbelief which reign even in the midst of the Christian nations, are we not driven to conclude that there is a need for manifest acts of the power of God to sustain the testimony of believers and to prove that God is with them? Besides, among believers themselves, how much of doubt, how much of weakness there is! How their faith needs to be awakened and stimulated by some evident proof of the presence of the Lord in their midst. One part of our being consists of flesh and blood; it is therefore in flesh and blood that God wills to manifest His presence.

In order to prove that it is the Church's unbelief which has lost the gift of healing, let us see what the Bible says about it. Does it not often put us on our guard against unbelief, against all which can estrange and turn us from our God? Does not the history of the Church show us the necessity of these warnings? Does it not furnish us with numerous examples of backward steps, of world pleasing, in which faith grew weak in the exact measure in which the spirit of the world took the upper hand? Faith is possible only to him who lives in the world invisible. Until the third century, the healings by faith in Christ were numerous, but in the centuries following they became more infrequent. Do we not know from the Bible that it is always unbelief which hinders the mighty working of God?

Oh, that we could learn to believe in the promises of God! God has not gone back from His promises; Jesus is still He who heals both soul and body; salvation offers us even now healing and holiness, and the Holy Spirit is always ready to give us some manifestations of His power. When we ask why this divine power is not more often seen, He answers us, "Because of your unbelief." The more we give ourselves to experience personally sanctification by faith, the more we shall also experience healing by faith. These two doctrines walk abreast. The more the Spirit of God lives and acts in the soul of believers, the more will the miracles multiply by which He works in the body. Thereby the world can recognize what redemption means.

Chapter 3
JESUS AND THE DOCTORS
(Mark 5:25-34)

We may be thankful to God for giving us doctors. Their vocation is one of the most noble, for a large number of them seek truly to do, with love and compassion, all they are able to alleviate the evils and sufferings which burden humanity as a result of sin. There are even some who are zealous servants of Jesus Christ, and who seek also the good of their patients' souls. Nevertheless, it is Jesus Himself who is always the first, the best, the greatest Physician.

Jesus heals diseases in which earthly physicians can do nothing, for the Father gave Him this power when He charged Him with the work of our redemption. Jesus, in taking upon Himself our human body, delivered it from the dominion of sin and Satan; He has made our bodies temples of the Holy Ghost, and members of His own body (I Cor. 6:15, 19). Even in our day, how many have been given up by the doctors as incurable, how many cases of cancer, of infection, of paralysis, of heart disease, of blindness, and of deafness, have been healed by Him! Is it not then astonishing that so small a number of the sick apply to Him?

The method of Jesus is quite different from that of earthly physicians. They seek to serve God in making use of remedies which are found in the natural world, and God makes use of these remedies according to the natural properties of each, while the healing which proceeds from Jesus is of a totally different order; it is by divine power, the power of the Holy Ghost, that Jesus heals. The difference between these two ways of healing is very marked. That we may understand it better, let us take an example: here is a physician who is an unbeliever, but extremely clever in his profession; many sick people owe their healing to him. God gives this result by means of the prescribed remedies, and the physician's knowledge of them. Here is another physician who is a believer, and who prays God's blessing on the remedies which he employs. In this case also, a large number are healed, but in neither case does the healing bring with it any spiritual blessing. They will be preoccupied, even the believing among them, with the remedies which they use much more than with what the Lord may be doing with them, and in such a case, their healing will be more hurtful than beneficial. On the other hand, when it is Jesus only to whom the sick person applies for healing, he learns to reckon no longer upon remedies, but to put himself into direct relation with His love and His almightiness. In order to obtain such healing, he must commence by confessing and renouncing his sins, and exercising a living faith. Then healing will come directly from the Lord, who takes possession of the sick body, and it thus becomes a blessing for the soul as well as for the body.

But is it not God who has given remedies to man? it is asked. Does not their power come from Him? Without doubt; but on the other hand, is it not God who has given us His Son with all power to heal? Shall we follow the way of natural law with all those who do not yet know Christ, and also with those of His children whose faith is still too weak to abandon themselves to His almightiness? Or rather do we choose the way of faith, receiving healing from the Lord and from the Holy Spirit, seeing therein the result and the proof of our redemption?

The healing which is wrought by our Lord Jesus brings with it and leaves behind it more real blessing than the healing which is obtained through physicians. Healing has been a misfortune to more persons than one. On a bed of sickness, serious thoughts had taken possession, but from the time of his healing, how often has a sick man been found anew far from the Lord! It is not thus when it is Jesus who heals. Healing is granted after confession of sin; therefore it brings the sufferer nearer to Jesus, and establishes a new link between him and the Lord. It causes him to experience His love and power, it begins within him a new life of faith and holiness. When the woman who had touched the hem of Christ's garment felt that she was healed, she learned something of what divine love means. She went away with the words, "Daughter, thy faith hath saved thee: go in peace" (Mark 5:34 ASV, margin).

O you who are suffering from some sickness, know that Jesus, the sovereign Healer, is yet in our midst. He is close to us, and He is giving anew to His Church manifest proofs of His presence. Are you ready to break with the

*world, to abandon yourself to Him with faith
and confidence? Then fear not. Remember
that divine healing is a part of the life of faith.
If nobody around you can help you in prayer,
if no "elder" is at hand to pray the prayer of
faith, fear not to go yourself to the Lord in the
silence of solitude, like the woman who
touched the hem of His garment. Commit to
Him the care of your body. Get quiet before
Him, and like the poor woman say, "I will be
healed." Perhaps it may take some time to
break the chains of your unbelief, but assuredly none that wait on Him shall be
ashamed (Ps. 25:3).*

Chapter 4

HEALTH AND SALVATION BY THE NAME OF JESUS

(Acts 3:16; 4:10, 12)

When, after Pentecost, the paralytic was healed through Peter and John at the gate of the temple, it was "in the name of Jesus Christ of Nazareth" that they said to him, "Rise up and walk," and as soon as the people in their amazement ran together to them, Peter declared that it was the name of Jesus which had so completely healed the man.

As the result of this miracle and of Peter's discourse, many people which had heard the Word believed (Acts 4:4). On the morrow, Peter repeated these words before the Sanhedrin: "By the name of Jesus Christ of Nazareth . . . doth this man stand here before you whole"; and then he added, "There is none other name under heaven . . . whereby we must be saved." This statement of Peter's declares to us that the name of Jesus both heals and saves. We have here a teaching of the highest import for divine healing.

We see that healing and health form part of Christ's salvation. Peter clearly states this in his discourse to the Sanhedrin where, having spoken of healing, he immediately goes on to speak of salvation by Christ (Acts 4:10, 12). In heaven, even our bodies will have their part in salvation; salvation will not be complete for us until our bodies enjoy the full redemption of Christ. Why then should we not believe in this work of redemption here below? Even already here on earth, the health of our bodies is a fruit of the salvation which Jesus has acquired for us.

We see also that health as well as salvation is to be obtained by faith. The tendency of man by nature is to bring about his salvation by his works, and it is only with difficulty that he comes to receive it by faith; but when it is a question of the healing of the body, he has still more difficulty in seizing it. As to salvation, he ends it by accepting it because by no other means can he open the door of heaven; while for the body, he makes use of well-known remedies. Why then should he seek for divine healing? Happy is he who comes to understand that it is the will of God to heal; to manifest the power of Jesus, and also to reveal to us His Fatherly love; to exercise and to confirm our faith, and to make us prove the power of redemption in the body as well as in the soul. The body is part of our being. Even the body has been saved by Christ; therefore, it is in our body that our Father wills to manifest the power of redemption, and to let men see that Jesus lives. Oh, let us believe in the name of Jesus! Was it not in the name of Jesus that perfect health was given to the crippled man? And were not words, "Thy faith hath saved thee," pronounced when the woman with the issue of blood was healed? Let us seek then to obtain divine healing.

Wherever the Spirit acts with power, there He works divine healings. Would it not seem that if ever miracles were superfluous, it was at Pentecost, for then the word of the apostles worked mightily, and the pouring out of the Holy Spirit was abundant? Well, it is precisely because the Spirit acted powerfully that His working must needs be visible in the body. If divine healing is seen but rarely in our day, we can attribute it to no other cause than that the Spirit does not act with power. The unbelief of worldlings and the want of zeal among believers stop His working. The healings which God is giving here and there are the precursory signs of all the spiritual graces which are promised to us, and it is only the Holy Spirit who reveals the almightiness of the name of Jesus to operate such healings. Let us pray earnestly for the Holy Spirit, let us place ourselves unreservedly under His direction, and let us seek to be firm in our faith in the name of Jesus, whether for preaching salvation or for the work of healing.

God grants healing to glorify the name of Jesus. Let us seek to be healed by Jesus that His name may be glorified. It is sad to see how little the power of His name is recognized, how little it is the end of preaching and of prayer. Treasures of divine grace, of which Christians deprive themselves by their lack of faith and zeal, are hidden in the name of Jesus. It is the will of God to glorify His Son in the Church, and He will do it wherever He finds faith. Whether among believers, or whether among the heathen, He is ready with virtue from on high to awaken consciences, and to bring hearts to obedience. God is ready to manifest the all-power of His Son, and to do it in a striking way in body as well as in soul. Let us believe it for ourselves, let us believe it for others, for the circle of believers around us, and also for the Church in the whole world. Let us give ourselves to believe with firm faith in the power of the name of Jesus. Let us ask great things in His name, counting on His promise, and we shall see God still do wonders by the name of His holy Son.

Chapter 5

NOT BY OUR OWN POWER

And when Peter saw it, he answered unto the people, Ye men of Israel why marvel ye at this? or why look ye so earnestly on us, as though by our own power or holiness we had made this man to walk? (Acts 3:12)

As soon as the crippled man had been healed at the gate of the temple, the people ran together to Peter and John. Peter, seeing this miracle was attributed to their power and holiness, lost no time in setting them right by telling them that all the glory of this miracle belonged to Jesus, and that it is He in whom we must believe.

Peter and John were undoubtedly full of faith and of holiness; they may have been the most holy and zealous servants of God in their time. Otherwise, God might not have chosen them as instruments in this case of healing. But they knew that their holiness of life was not of themselves, that it was of God through the Holy Spirit. They thought so little of themselves that they ignored their own holiness and know only one thing—that all power belongs to their Master. They hastened, then, to declare that in this thing they counted for nothing, that it was the work of the Lord alone. This is the object of divine healing, to be a proof of the power of Jesus, a witness in the eyes of men of what He is, proclaiming His divine intervention, and attracting hearts to Him. "Not by our own power or holiness." Thus it becomes those to speak whom the Lord is pleased to use in helping others by their faith.

It is necessary to insist on this because of the tendency of believers to think the contrary. Those who have recovered their health in answer to "the prayer of faith," "the supplication of a righteous man availeth much in its working" (James 5:16 RV), are in danger of being too much occupied with the human instrument which God is pleased to employ, and to think that the power lies in man's piety.

Doubtless the prayer of faith is the result of real godliness, but those who possess it will be the first to acknowledge that it does not come from themselves, nor from any effort of their own. They fear to rob the Lord of the least particle of the glory which belongs to Him, and they know that if they do so, they will compel Him to withdraw His grace from them. It is their great desire to see the souls which God has blessed through them enter into a direct and increasingly intimate communion with the Lord Jesus Christ Himself, since that is the result which their healing should produce. Thus they insist that it is not caused by their own power or holiness.

Such testimony on their part is necessary to reply to the erroneous accusations of unbelievers. The Church of Christ needs to hear clearly announced that it is on account of her worldliness and unbelief that she has lost these spiritual gifts of healing (I Cor. 12:9) and that the Lord restores those gifts to those who, with faith and obedience, have consecrated their lives to Him. This grace cannot reappear without being preceded by a renewal of faith and of holiness. But then, says the world, and with it a large number of Christians, "You are laying claim to the possession of a higher order of faith and holiness; you consider yourselves holier than others." To such accusations, this word of Peter is the only reply before God and before man, confirmed by a life of deep and real humility:

"Not by our own power or holiness." "Not unto us, O Lord, not unto us, but unto thy name give glory, for thy mercy, and for thy truth's sake" (Ps. 115:1).

Such a testimony is necessary also in view of our own heart and of the wiles of Satan. As long as, through the Church's unfaithfulness, the gifts of healing are but rarely given, those children of God who have received these gifts are in danger of priding themselves upon them, and of imagining that they have in themselves something exceptionally meritorious. The enemy does not forget to persecute them by such insinuations, and woe unto them if they listen to him. They are not ignorant of his devices; therefore, they need to pray continually to the Lord to keep them in humility, the true means of obtaining continually more grace. If they persevere in humility, they will recognize that the more God makes use of them, the more also will they be penetrated with the conviction that it is God alone who works by them, and that all the glory belongs to Him. "Not I, but the grace of God which was with me" (I Cor. 15:10). Such is their watchword.

Finally, this testimony is useful for the feeble ones who long for salvation, and who desire to receive Christ as their Healer. They hear of full consecration and entire obedience, but they form a false idea of it. They think they must in themselves attain to a high degree of knowledge and of perfection, and they fall a prey to discouragement. No, no; it is not by our own power or holiness that we obtain these graces, but by a faith quite simple, a childlike faith, which knows that it has no power nor holiness of its own, and which commits itself completely to Him who is faithful, and whose almightiness can fulfill His promise. Oh, let us not seek to do or to be anything of ourselves! It is only as we feel our own powerlessness, and expect all from God and His Word that we realize the glorious way in which the Lord heals sickness by faith in His name.

Chapter 6

ACCORDING TO THE MEASURE OF FAITH

And Jesus said unto the centurion, Go thy way; and as thou hast believed, so be it done unto thee. And his servant was healed in the selfsame hour. (Matt. 8:13)

This passage of Scripture brings before us one of the principal laws of the kingdom of heaven. In order to understand God's ways with His people, and our relations with the Lord, it is needful to understand this law thoroughly and not to deviate from it. Not only does God give or withhold His grace according to the faith or unbelief of each, but it is granted in greater or lesser measure, in proportion to the faith which receives it. God respects the right to decide which He has conferred on man. Therefore He can bless us only in the measure in which each yields himself up to His divine working, and opens all his heart to Him. Faith in God is nothing else than the full opening of the heart to receive everything from God; therefore, man can receive divine grace only according to his faith; and this applies as much to divine healing as to any other grace of God.

This truth is confirmed by the spiritual blessings which may result from sickness. Two questions are often asked: (1) Is it not God's will that His children should sometimes remain in a prolonged state of sickness? (2) Since it is a recognized thing that divine healing brings with it greater spiritual blessing than the sickness itself, why does God allow certain of His children to continue sick through many years, and while in this condition give them blessing in sanctification and in communion with Himself? The answer to these two questions is that God gives to His children according to their faith. We have already had occasion to remark that in the same degree in which the Church has become worldly, her faith in divine healing has diminished until at last it has disappeared. Believers do not seem to be aware that they may ask God for the healing of their sickness, and that thereby they may be sanctified and fitted for His service. They have come to seek only submission to His will and to regard sickness as a means to be separate from the world. In such conditions, the Lord gives them what they ask. He would have been ready to give them yet more, to grant them healing in answer to the prayer of faith, but they lacked the faith to receive it. God always meets His children where they are, however weak they may be. The sick ones, therefore, who have desired to receive Him with their whole heart, will have received from Him the fruit of the sickness in their desire that their will should be conformed to the will of God. They might have been able to receive healing, in addition, as a proof that God accepted their submission; if this has not been so, it is because faith has failed them to ask for it.

"As thou hast believed so be it done unto thee." These words give the reply to yet another question: How can you say that divine healing brings with it so much of spiritual blessing, when one sees that the greater number of those who were healed by the Lord Jesus received nothing more than a deliverance from their present sufferings, without giving any proof that they were also spiritually blest? Here again, as they believed, so was it done unto them.

A good number of sick people, having witnessed the healing of others, gained confidence in Jesus just far enough to be healed, and Jesus granted them their request, without adding other blessings for their souls. Before His ascension, the Lord had not as free an entrance as He now has into the heart of man, because "the Holy Ghost was not yet given" (John 7:39). The healing of the sick was then hardly more than a blessing for the body. It was only later, in the dispensation of the Spirit, that the conviction and confession of sin have become for the believer the first grace to be received, the essential condition for obtaining healing, as Saint Paul tells us in his Epistle to the Corinthians, and James in his to the twelve tribes scattered abroad (I Cor. 11:31-32; James 5:16). Thus the degrees of spiritual grace which it is possible for us to receive depend upon the measure of our faith, whether it be for its external manifestation, or for its influence upon our inner life.

We commend then to every suffering one who is looking for healing, and seeks to know Jesus as his divine Healer, not to let himself be hindered by his unbelief, not to doubt the promises of God, but to be strong in faith, giving glory to God as is His due. "As thou hast believed, so be it done unto thee." If with all your heart you trust in the living God, you will be abundantly blessed. Do not doubt it.

The part of faith is always to lay hold on just that which appears impossible or strange to human eyes. Let us be willing to be considered fools for Christ's sake (I Cor. 4:10). Let us not fear to pass for weak-minded in the eyes of the world and of such Christians as are ignorant of these things, because, on the authority of the Word of God, we believe that which others cannot yet admit. Do not, then, let yourself be discouraged in your expectation, even though God should delay to answer you, or if your sickness be aggravated. Once having placed your foot firmly on the immovable rock of God's own Word, and having prayed the Lord to manifest His almightiness in your body because you are one of the members of His Body, and the temple of the Holy Ghost, persevere in believing in Him with the firm assurance that He has undertaken for you, that He has made Himself responsible for your body, and that His healing virtue will come to glorify Him in you.

Chapter 7

THE WAY OF FAITH

And straightway the father of the child cried out, and said with tears, Lord, I believe; help thou mine unbelief. (Mark 9:24)

These words have been a help and strength to thousands of souls in their pursuit of salvation and the gifts of God. Notice that it is in relation to an afflicted child that they were pronounced, in the fight of faith when seeking healing from the Lord Jesus. In them, we see that in one and the same soul there can arise a struggle between faith and unbelief, and that it is not without a struggle that we come to believe in Jesus and in His all-power to heal the sick. In this we find the needful encouragement for realizing the Savior's power.

I speak here especially to sufferers who do not doubt the power or the will of the Lord Jesus to heal in this day without the use of earthly remedies, but who lack the boldness to accept healing for themselves. They believe in the divine power of Christ, they believe in a general manner His good will to heal; they have acquired, either by the Scriptures, or by facts of healings by the Lord alone which have taken place in our days, the intellectual persuasion that the Lord can help even them, but they shrink back from accepting healing, and from saying with faith, "The Lord has heard me. I know that He is healing me."

Take notice first that without faith no one can be healed. When the father of the afflicted child said to Jesus, "If thou canst do anything, have compassion on us, and help us," Jesus replied, "If *thou* canst believe." Jesus had the power to heal, and He was ready to do it, but He cast responsibility on the man. "If *thou* canst. All things are possible to him that believeth" (RV). In order to obtain your healing from Jesus, it is not enough to pray. Prayer without faith is powerless. It is "the prayer of faith" which saves the sick (James 5:15). If you have already asked for healing from the Lord, or if others have asked it for you, you must, before you are conscious of any change, be able to say with faith, "On the authority of God's Word, I have the assurance that He hears me and that I shall be healed." To have faith means in your case to surrender your body absolutely into the Lord's hands, and to leave yourself entirely to Him. Faith receives healing as a spiritual grace which proceeds from the Lord, even while there is no conscious change in the body. Faith can glorify God and say, "Bless the Lord, O my soul . . . who healeth all my diseases" (Ps. 103:1-3). The Lord requires this faith that He may heal.

But how is such faith to be obtained? Tell your God the unbelief which you find in your heart, and count on Him for deliverance from it. Faith is not money by which your healing can be purchased from the Lord. It is He who desires to awaken and develop in you the necessary faith. "Help my unbelief," cried the father of the child. It was his ardent desire that his faith should not come short. Confess to the Lord all the difficulty you have to believe Him on the ground of His Word; tell Him you want to be rid of this unbelief, that you bring it to Him with a will to hearken only to His Word. Do not lose time in deploring your unbelief, but look to Jesus. The light of His countenance will enable you to find the power to believe in Him (Ps. 43:3). He calls on you to trust in Him. Listen to Him, and by

His grace, faith will triumph in you. Say to Him, "Lord, I am still aware of the unbelief which is in me. I find it difficult to believe that I am sure of my healing because I possess Him who works it. And, nevertheless, I want to conquer this unbelief. Thou, Lord, wilt give me the victory. I desire to believe, I will believe, by Thy grace, I dare to say I can believe. Yes, Lord, I believe, for Thou comest to the help of my unbelief." It is when we are in intimate communion with the Lord, and when our heart responds to His, that unbelief is overcome and conquered.

It is needful also to testify to the faith one has. Be resolved to believe that which the Lord says to you, to believe, above all, that which He is. Lean wholly upon His promises. "The prayer of faith shall save the sick." "I am the Lord that healeth thee" (Exod. 15:26). Look to Jesus, who "bare our sicknesses" (Matt. 8:17), and who healed all who came to Him. Count on the Holy Spirit to manifest in your heart the presence of Jesus who is also now in heaven, and to work also in your body the power of His grace. Praise the Lord without waiting to feel better, or to have more faith. Praise Him, and say with David, "O Lord, my God, I cried unto thee, and thou hast healed me" (Ps. 30:2). Divine healing is a spiritual grace which can only be received spiritually and by faith, before feeling its effect on the body. Accept it, then, and give glory to God. When the Lord Jesus had commanded the unclean spirit to come out of the child, he rent him sore, so that he was as one dead, inasmuch as many said, "He is dead." If, therefore, your sickness does not yield at once, if Satan and your own unbelief attempt to get the upper hand, do not heed them. Cling closely to Jesus your Healer, and He will surely heal you.

Chapter 8

YOUR BODY IS THE TEMPLE OF THE HOLY GHOST

(I Cor. 6:15, 19-20)

The Bible teaches us that the Body of Christ is the company of the faithful. These words are taken generally in their spiritual sense, while the Bible asks us positively whether we know not that our bodies are the members of Christ. In the same way, when the Bible speaks of the indwelling of the Holy Spirit or of Christ, we limit His presence to the spiritual part of our being. Nevertheless, the Bible says expressly, "Know ye not that your *body* is a temple of the Holy Spirit?" (ASV). When the Church understands that the body also has part in the redemption which is by Christ, by which it ought to be brought back to its original destiny, to be the dwelling place of the Holy Spirit, to serve as His instrument, to be sanctified by His presence, she will also recognize all the place which divine healing has in the Bible and in the counsels of God.

The account of the creation tells us that man is composed of three parts. God first formed the body from the dust of the earth, after which He breathed into it "the breath of life." He caused His own life, His Spirit, to enter into it. By this union of Spirit with matter, the man became a "living soul." The soul, which is essentially the man, finds its place between the body and the spirit; it is the link which binds them together. By the body, the soul finds itself in relation to the external world; by the spirit, with the world invisible and with God. By means of the soul, the spirit can subject the body to the action of the heavenly powers and thus spiritualize it; by means of the soul, the body also can act upon the spirit and attract it earthward. The soul, subject to the solicitations of both spirit and body, is in a position to choose between the voice of God, speaking by the spirit, or the voice of the world, speaking through the senses.

This union of spirit and body forms a combination which is unique in the creation; it makes man to be the jewel of God's work. Other creatures had existed already; some were like angels, all spirit, without any material body; and others, like the animals, were only flesh, possessing a body animated with a living soul, but devoid of spirit. Man was destined to show that the material body, governed by the spirit, was capable of being transformed by the power of the Spirit of God, and of being thus led to participate in heavenly glory.

We know what sin and Satan have done with this possibility of gradual transformation. By means of the body, the spirit was tempted, seduced, and became a slave of sense. We know also what God has done to destroy the work of Satan and to accomplish the purpose of creation. "The Son of God was manifested that He might destroy the works of the devil" (I John 3:8). God prepared a body for His Son (Heb. 10:5). "The Word was made flesh" (John 1:14). "In Him dwelleth all the fulness of the Godhead bodily" (Col. 2:9). "Who his own self bare our sins in his own body on the tree" (I Peter 2:24). And now Jesus, raised up from the dead with a body as free from sin as His spirit and His soul, communicates to our body the virtue of His glorified body. The Lord's Supper is "the communion of the body of Christ"; and our bodies are "the members of Christ" (I Cor. 10:16; 6:15; 12:27).

Faith puts us in possession of all that the death of Christ and His resurrection have procured for us, and it is not only in our spirit and our soul that the life of the risen Jesus manifests its presence here below, it is in the body also that it would act according to the measure of our faith.

"Know ye not that your body is the temple of the Holy Spirit?" Many believers represent to themselves that the Holy Spirit comes to dwell in our body as we dwell in a house. Nothing of the kind. I can dwell in a house without its becoming part of my being. I may leave it without suffering; no vital union exists between my house and me. It is not thus with the presence of our soul and spirit in our body. The life of a plant lives and animates every part of it; and our soul is not limited to dwell in such or such part of the body, the heart or the head, for instance, but penetrates throughout, even to the end of the lowest members. The life of the soul pervades the whole body; the life throughout proves the presence of the soul. It is in like manner that the Holy Ghost comes to dwell in our body. He penetrates its entirety. He animates and possesses us infinitely more than we can imagine.

In the same way in which the Holy Spirit brings to our soul and spirit the life of Jesus, His holiness, His joy, His strength, He comes also to impart to the sick body all the vigorous vitality of Christ as soon as the hand of faith is stretched out to receive it. When the body is fully subject to Christ, crucified with Him, renouncing all self-will and independence, desiring nothing but to be the Lord's temple, it is then that the Holy Spirit manifests the power of the risen Savior in the body. Then only can we glorify God in our body, leaving Him full freedom to manifest therein His power, to show that He knows how to set His temple free from the domination of sickness, sin, and Satan.

Chapter 9

THE BODY FOR THE LORD

(I Cor. 6:13)

One of the most learned of theologians has said that the redemption and glorification of the body is the end of the ways of God.

As we have already seen, this is indeed what God has accomplished in creating man. It is this which makes the inhabitants of heaven wonder and admire when they contemplate the glory of the Son. Clothed with a human body, Jesus has taken His place forever upon the throne of God, to partake of His glory. It is this which God has willed. It shall be recognized in that day when regenerated humanity, forming the Body of Christ, shall be truly and visibly the temple of the living God (I Cor. 6:19), and when all creation in the new heavens and new earth shall share the glory of the children of God. The material body shall then be wholly sanctified, glorified by the Spirit; and this body, thus spiritualized, shall be the highest glory of the Lord Jesus Christ and of His redeemed.

It is in anticipation of this new condition of things that the Lord attaches a great importance to the indwelling and sanctification of our bodies, down here, by His Spirit. So little is this truth understood by believers that less still do they seek for the power of the Holy Spirit in their bodies. Many of them also, believing that this body belongs to them, use it as it pleases them. Not understanding how much the sanctification of the soul and spirit depends upon the body, they do not grasp all the meaning of the words, "The body is for the Lord," in such a way as to receive them in obedience.

"The body is for the Lord." What does this mean? The apostle has just said, "Meats for the belly, and the belly for meats; but God shall destroy both it and them." Eating and drinking afford the Christian an opportunity of carrying out this truth, "The body is for the Lord." He must indeed learn to eat and drink to the glory of God. By eating, sin and the Fall came about. It was also through eating that the devil sought to tempt our Lord. Thus

Jesus Himself sanctified His body in eating only according to the will of His Father (Matt. 4:4). Many believers fail to watch over their bodies, to observe a holy sobriety through the fear of rendering it unfit for the service of God. Eating and drinking should never impede communion with God; its end is, on the contrary, to facilitate it in maintaining the body in its normal condition.

The apostle speaks also of fornication, this sin which defiles the body, and which is in direct opposition to the words, "The body is for the Lord." It is not simply incontinence outside the married state, but in that state also, which is meant here; all voluptuousness, all want of sobriety of whatsoever kind is condemned in these words: "Your body is the temple of the Holy Ghost" (I Cor. 6:19). In the same way, all of what goes to maintain the body—to clothe it, strengthen it, rest it in sleep, or afford it enjoyment—should be placed under the control of the Holy Spirit. As under the Old Covenant the temple was constructed solely for God, and for His service, even so our body has been created for the Lord and for Him alone.

One of the chief benefits then of divine healing will be to teach us that our body ought to be set free from the yoke of our own will to become the Lord's property. God does not grant healing to our prayers until He has attained the end for which He had permitted the sickness. He wills that this discipline should bring us into a more intimate communion with Him; He would make us understand that we have regarded our body as our own property, while it belonged to the Lord; and that the Holy Spirit seeks to sanctify all its actions. He leads us to understand that if we yield our body unreservedly to the influence of the Holy Spirit, we shall experience His power in us, and He will heal us by bringing into our body the very life of Jesus. He leads us, in short, to say with full conviction, "The body is for the Lord."

There are believers who seek after holiness, but only for the soul and spirit. In their ignorance, they forget that the body and all its systems of nerves; that the hand, the ear, the eyes, the mouth are called to testify directly to the presence and the grace of God in them. They have not sufficiently taken in these words: "Your bodies are the members of Christ" (I Cor. 6:15). "If by the Spirit ye make to die the deeds of the body, ye shall live" (Rom. 8:13 RV, margin). "The God of peace himself sanctify you wholly, and may your spirit and soul and body be preserved entire, without blame, at the coming of our Lord Jesus Christ" (I Thess. 5:23 ASV). Oh, what a renewing takes place in us when, by His own touch, the Lord heals our bodies, when He takes possession of them, and when by His Spirit He becomes life and health to them! It is with an indescribable consciousness of holiness, of fear, and of joy that the believer can then offer his body a living sacrifice to receive healing, and to have for his motto these words: "The body is for the Lord."

Chapter 10

THE LORD FOR THE BODY

(I Cor. 6:13)

There is reciprocity in God's relations with
man. That which God has been for me, I
ought in my turn to be for Him. And that
which I am for Him, He desires again to be
for me. If, in His love, He gives Himself fully
to me, it is in order that I may lovingly give
myself fully to Him. In the measure in which
I more or less really surrender to Him all my
being, in that measure also He gives Himself
more really to me. God thus leads the believer
to understand that this abandonment of Himself comprises the body, and the more our life
bears witness that that body is for the Lord,
the more also we experience that the Lord is
for the body. In saying, "The body is for the
Lord," we express the desire to regard our

body as wholly consecrated, offered in sacrifice to the Lord, and sanctified by Him. In saying, "The Lord is for the body," we express the precious certainty that our offering has been accepted, and that, by His Spirit, the Lord will impart to our body His own strength and holiness, and that henceforth He will strengthen and keep us.

This is a matter of faith. Our body is material, weak, feeble, sinful, mortal. Therefore, it is difficult to grasp all at once the full extent of the words, "The Lord is for the body." It is the Word of God which explains to us the way to assimilate. The body was created by the Lord and for the Lord. Jesus took upon Him an earthly body. In His body, He bore our sins on the cross, and thereby set our body free from the power of sin. In Christ, the body has been raised again, and seated on the throne of God. The body is the habitation of the Holy Spirit; it is called to eternal partnership in the glory of heaven. Therefore, with certainty, and in a wide and universal sense, we can say, "Yes, the Lord Jesus, our Savior, is for the body."

This truth has various applications. In the first place, it is a great help in practical holiness. More than one sin derives its strength from some physical tendency. The converted drunkard has a horror of intoxicating drinks, but, notwithstanding, his appetites are sometimes a snare to him, gaining victory over his new convictions. If, however, in the conflict, he gives over his body with confidence to the Lord, all physical appetite, all desire to drink will be overcome. Our temper also often results from our physical constitution. A nervous, irritable system produces words which are sharp, harsh, and wanting in love. But let the body with this physical tendency be taken to the Lord, and it will soon be experienced that the Holy Spirit can mortify the risings of impatience, and sanctify the body, rendering it blameless.

These words, "The Lord is for the body," are applicable also to the physical strength which the Lord's service demands of us. When David cries, "It is God that girdeth me with strength," he means physical strength, for he adds, "He maketh my feet like hinds' feet . . . mine arms do bend a bow of brass"(Ps. 18:32-34). Again in these words, "The Lord is the strength of my life" (Ps. 27:1), it does not mean only the spiritual man, but the entire man. Many believers have experienced that the promise, "They that wait upon the Lord shall renew their strength" (Isa. 40:31) touches the body, and that the

Holy Spirit increases their physical strength.

But it is especially in divine healing that we see the truth of these words, "The Lord is for the body." Yes, Jesus, the sovereign and merciful Healer, is always ready to save and cure. There was in Switzerland, some years ago, a young girl near death from tuberculosis. The doctor had advised a milder climate, but she was too weak to take the journey. She learned that Jesus is the Healer of the sick. She believed the good news, and one night when she was thinking of this subject, it seemed to her that the Body of the Lord drew near to her, and that she ought to take these words literally, "His body for our body." From this moment, she began to improve. Some time after, she began to hold Bible readings, and later on she became a zealous and much-blessed worker for the Lord among women. She had learned to understand that the Lord is for the body.

Dear sick one, the Lord has shown you by sickness what power sin has over the body. By your healing, He would also show you the power of redemption of the body. He calls you to show that which you have not understood until now, that "the body is for the Lord." Therefore, give Him your body. Give it to Him with your sickness and your sin, which is the original source of sickness. Believe always that the Lord has taken charge of this body, and He will manifest with power that He really is the Lord, who is for the body. The Lord, who has Himself taken upon Him a body here on earth and regenerated it, from the highest heaven, where He now is, clothed with His glorified body, sends us His divine strength, willing thus to manifest His power in our body.

Chapter 11

DO NOT CONSIDER YOUR BODY

(Rom. 6:19-21)

When God promised Abraham to give him a son, the patriarch would never have been able to believe in this promise if he had considered his own body, already aged and worn out. But Abraham would see nothing but God and His promise, the power and faithfulness of God who guaranteed him the fulfilment of His promise.

This enables us to lay hold of all the difference there is between the healing which is expected from earthly remedies and the healing which is looked for from God only. When we have recourse to remedies for healing, all the attention of the sick one is upon the body, considering the body, while divine healing calls us to turn our attention away from the body, and to abandon ourselves, soul and body, to the Lord's care, occupying ourselves with Him alone.

This truth equally enables us to see the difference between the sickness retained for blessing and the healing received from the Lord. Some are afraid to take the promise in James 5 in its literal sense, because they say sickness is more profitable to the soul than health. It is true that in the case of healing obtained by earthly remedies, many people would be more blessed in remaining ill than in recovering health, but it is quite otherwise when healing comes directly from the hand of God. In order to receive divine healing, sin must be so truly confessed and renounced, one must be so completely surrendered to the Lord, self must be so really yielded up to be wholly in His hands, and the will of Jesus to take charge of the body must be so firmly counted on that the healing becomes the commencement of a new life of intimate communion with the Lord.

Thus we learn to give up to Him entirely the care of the health, and the smallest indication of the return of the evil is regarded as a warning not to consider our body, but to be occupied with the Lord only.

What a contrast this is from the greater

number of sick people who look for healing from remedies. If some few of them have been sanctified by the sickness, having learned to lose sight of themselves, how many more are there who are drawn by the sickness itself to be constantly occupied with themselves and with the condition of their body. What infinite care they exercise in observing the least symptom, favorable or unfavorable! What a constant preoccupation to them is their eating and drinking, the anxiety to avoid this or that! How much they are taken up with what they consider due to them from others, whether they are sufficiently thought of, whether well enough nursed, whether visited often enough! How much time is thus devoted to considering the body and what it exacts, rather than the Lord and the relations which He seeks to establish with their souls! Oh, how many are they who, through sickness, are occupied almost exclusively with themselves!

All this is totally different when healing is looked for in faith from the loving God. Then the first thing to learn is to cease to be anxious about the state of your body; you have trusted it to the Lord, and He has taken the responsibility. If you do not see a rapid improvement immediately, but on the contrary the symptoms appear to be more serious, remember that you have entered on a path of faith, and therefore you ought not to consider the body, but cling only to the living God. The commandment of Christ, "Be not anxious for your . . . body" (Matt. 6:25 ASV), appears here in a new light. When God called Abraham not to consider his own body, it was that He might call him to the greatest exercise of faith which could be, that he might learn to see only God and His promise. Sustained by his faith, he gave glory to God, convinced that God would do what He had promised. Divine healing is a marvelous tie to bind us to the Lord. At first, one may fear to believe that the Lord will stretch forth His mighty hand and touch the body; but in studying the Word of God, the soul takes courage and confidence. At last one decides, saying, "I yield up my body into the hands of God; and I leave the care of it to Him." Then the body and its sensations are lost sight of, and only the Lord and His promise are in view.

Dear reader, will you also enter upon this way of faith, very superior to that which it is the habit to call natural? Walk in the steps of Abraham. Learn from him not to consider your own body, and not to doubt through unbelief. To consider the body gives birth to doubts, while clinging to the promise of God and being occupied with Him alone gives entrance into the way of faith, the way of divine healing, which glorifies God.

Chapter 12

DISCIPLINE AND SANCTIFICATION

God . . . chasteneth . . . us . . . for our profit, that we may be partakers of his holiness. (Heb. 12:7, 10)

If a man . . . purge himself . . . he shall be a vessel unto honour, sanctified and meet for the master's use, and prepared unto every good work. (II Tim. 2:21)

To sanctify anything is to set it apart, to consecrate it, to God and to His service. The temple at Jerusalem was holy, that is to say, it was consecrated, dedicated to God that it might serve Him as a dwelling place. The vessels of the temple were holy, because they were devoted to the service of the temple; the priests were holy, chosen to serve God and ready to work for Him. In the same way, the Christian ought also to be sanctified, at the Lord's disposal, ready to do every good work.

When the people of Israel went out of Egypt, the Lord reclaimed them for His service as a holy people. "Let my people go, that they may serve me" (Exod. 7:16), He said to Pharaoh. Set free from their hard bondage, the children of Israel were debtors to enter at once upon the service of God, and to become His happy servants. Their deliverance was the road which led to their sanctification.

Again in this day, God is forming for Himself a holy people, and Jesus sets us free that we may form part of them. He "gave himself for us, that he might redeem us from all iniquity, and purify unto himself a people for his own possession, zealous of good works" (Titus 2:14 ASV). It is the Lord who breaks the chains by which Satan would hold us in bondage. He would have us free, wholly free to serve Him. He wills to save us, to deliver both the soul and the body, that each of the members of the body may be consecrated to Him and placed unreservedly at His disposal.

A large number of Christians do not yet understand all this; they do not know how to take in that the purpose of their deliverance is that they may be sanctified, prepared to serve their God. They make use of their life and their members to procure their own satisfaction; consequently, they do not feel at liberty to ask for healing with faith. It is therefore to chasten them—that they may be brought to desire sanctification—that the Lord permits Satan to inflict sickness upon them, and by it keeps them chained and prisoners (Luke 13:11,16). God chastens us "for our profit, that we may be partakers of his holiness" (Heb. 12:10), and that we may be sanctified, "meet for the master's use" (II Tim. 2:21).

The discipline which the sickness inflicts brings great blessings with it. It is a call to the sick one to reflect; it leads him to see that God is occupied with him, and seeks to show him what there is which still separates him from Himself. God speaks to him; He calls him to examine His ways, to acknowledge that he has lacked holiness, and that the purpose of the chastisement is to make him partaker of His holiness. He awakens within him the desire to be enlightened by the Holy Spirit down into the inmost recesses of his heart, that he may be enabled to get a clear idea of what his life has been up to the present time, a life of self-will, very unlike the holy life which God requires of him. He leads him to confess his sins, to entrust them to the Lord Jesus, to believe that the Savior can deliver him from them. He urges him to yield to Him, to consecrate his life to Him, to die to himself that he may be able to live unto God.

Sanctification is not something which you can accomplish yourself; it cannot even be produced by God in you as something which you can possess and contemplate in yourself. No, it is the Holy Spirit, the Spirit of holiness alone who can communicate His holiness to you and renew it continually. Therefore it is by faith you can become partakers of His holiness. Having understood that Jesus has been made unto you of God sanctification (I Cor. 1:30), and that it is the Holy Spirit's work to impart to you His holiness which was manifested in His life on earth, surrender yourself to Him by faith that He may enable you to live that life from hour to hour. Believe that the Lord will by His Spirit lead you into, and keep you in, this life of holiness and of consecration to God's service. Live thus in the obedience of faith, always attentive to His voice, and the guidance of His Spirit.

From the time that this Fatherly discipline has led the sick one to a life of holiness, God has attained His purpose, and He will heal him who asks it in faith. Our earthly parents "for a few days chastened us. . . . All chastening seemeth for the present to be not joyous, but grievous, yet afterward it yieldeth the peaceable fruit of righteousness unto them that have been exercised thereby" (Heb. 12: 10-11 RV). Yes, it is when the believer realizes this "peaceable fruit of righteousness," that he is in a condition to be delivered from the chastisement.

Oh, it is because believers still understand so little that sanctification means an entire consecration to God that they cannot really believe that healing will quickly follow the sanctification of the sick one. Good health is too often for them only a matter of personal comfort and enjoyment which they may dispose of at their will, but God cannot thus minister to their selfishness. If they understood better that God requires of His children that they should be "sanctified and meet for the master's use," they would not be surprised to see Him giving healing and renewed strength to those who have learned to place all their members at His disposal, willing to be sanctified and employed in His service by the Holy Spirit. The Spirit of healing is also the Spirit of sanctification.

Chapter 13

SICKNESS AND DEATH

(Ps. 91:3, 5-6, 16; 92:14)

This objection is often made to the words of the apostle James, "The prayer of faith shall save the sick": If we have the promise of being always healed in answer to prayer, how can it be possible to die? And some add: How can a sick person know whether God, who fixes the time of our life, has not decided that we shall die by such a sickness? In such a case, would not prayer be useless, and would it not be a sin to ask for healing?

Before replying, we would remark that this objection touches not such as believe in Jesus as the Healer of the sick, but the Word of God itself, and the promise so clearly declared in the epistle of James and elsewhere. We are not at liberty to change or to limit the promises of God whenever they present some difficulty to us; neither can we insist that they shall be clearly explained to us before we can bring ourselves to believe what they state. It is for us to begin by receiving them without resistance; then only can the Spirit of God find us in the state of mind in which we can be taught and enlightened.

Furthermore, we would remark that in considering a divine truth which has been for a long time neglected in the Church, it can hardly be understood at the outset. It is only little by little that its importance and bearing are discerned. Gradually, as it revives, after it has been accepted by faith, the Holy Spirit will accompany it with new light. Let us remember that it is by the unbelief of the Church that divine healing has left her. It is not on the answers of such or such an one that faith in Bible truths should be made to depend. "There ariseth light in the darkness" (Ps. 112:4) for the "upright" who are ready to submit themselves to the Word of God.

1. To the first objection, it is easy to reply. Scripture fixes seventy or eighty years as the ordinary measure of human life. The believer who receives Jesus as the Healer of the sick will rest satisfied then with the declaration of the Word of God. He will feel at liberty to ex-

pect a life of seventy years, but not longer. Besides, the man of faith places himself under the direction of the Spirit, which will enable him to discern the will of God regarding him, if something should prevent his attaining the age of seventy. Every rule has its exceptions, in the things of heaven as in the things of earth. Of this, therefore, we are sure according to the Word of God, whether by the words of Jesus or by those of James, that our heavenly Father wills, as a rule, to see His children in good health that they may labor in His service. For the same reason, He wills to set them free from sickness as soon as they have made confession of sin and prayed with faith for their healing. For the believer who has walked with his Savior, strong with the strength which proceeds from divine healing, and whose body is consequently under the influence of the Holy Spirit, it is not necessary that when his time comes to die, he should die of sickness. To "fall asleep in Jesus Christ," such is the death of the believer when the end of his life is come. For him, death is only sleep after fatigue, the entering into rest. The promise, "That it may be well with thee, and that thou mayest live long on the earth" (Eph. 6:3) is addressed to us who live under the New Covenant. The more the believer has learned to see in the Savior Him who "took our infirmities," the more he has the liberty to claim the literal fulfilment of the promises: "With long life will I satisfy him" (Ps. 91:16); "They shall bring forth fruit in old age, they shall be fat and flourishing" (Ps. 92:14).

2. The same text applies to the second objection. The sick one sees in God's Word that it is His will to heal His children after the confession of their sins, and in answer to the prayer of faith. It does not follow that they shall be exempt from other trials; but as for sickness, they are healed of it because it attacks the body, which has become the dwelling place of the Holy Spirit. The sick one should then desire healing that the power of God may be made manifest in him, and that he may serve Him in accomplishing His will. In this, he clings to the revealed will of God, and for that which is not revealed, he knows that God will make known His mind to His servants who walk with Him. We would insist here that faith is not a logical reasoning which ought in some way to oblige God to act according to His promises. It is rather the confident attitude of the child who honors his Father, who counts upon His love, to see Him fulfilling His promises, and who knows that He is faithful to communicate to the body as

well as to the soul the new strength which flows from the redemption, until the moment of departure is come.

Chapter 14

THE HOLY SPIRIT
THE SPIRIT OF HEALING

(I Cor. 12:4, 9, 11)

What is it which distinguishes the children of God? What is their glory? It is that God dwells in the midst of them and reveals Himself to them in power (Exod. 33:16; 34:9-10). Under the New Covenant, this dwelling of God in the believer is still more manifest than in former times. God sends the Holy Spirit to His Church, which is the Body of Christ, to act in her with power, and her life and her prosperity depend on Him. The Spirit must find in her unreserved, full liberty, that she may be recognized as the Church of Christ, the Lord's Body. In every age, the Church may look for manifestations of the Spirit, for they form our indissoluble unity: "one body and one Spirit" (Eph. 4:4).

The Spirit operates variously in such or such a member of the Church. It is possible to be filled with the Spirit for one special work and not for another. There are also times in the history of the Church when certain gifts of the Spirit are given with power, while at the same time ignorance or unbelief may hinder other gifts. Wherever the life more abundant of the Spirit is to be found, we may expect Him to manifest all His gifts.

The gift of healing is one of the most beautiful manifestations of the Spirit. It is recorded of Jesus, "how God anointed Jesus of Nazareth . . . who went about doing good, and healing all that were oppressed of the devil" (Acts 10:38). The Holy Spirit in Him was a healing Spirit, and He was the same in the disciples after Pentecost. Thus the words of our text express what was the continuous experience of the early churches (compare attentively Acts 3:7; 4:30; 5:12, 15-16; 6:8; 8:7; 9:41; 14:9-10; 16:18-19; 19:12; 28:8-9). The abundant pouring out of the Spirit produced abundant healings. What a lesson for the Church in our days!

Divine healing is the work of the Holy Spirit. Christ's redemption extends its powerful working to the body, and the Holy Spirit is in charge of transmitting it to us and maintaining it in us. Our body shares in the benefit of the redemption, and even now it can receive the pledge of it by divine healing. It is Jesus who heals, Jesus who anoints and baptizes with the Holy Spirit, Jesus who baptized His disciples with the same Spirit. It is He who sends us the Holy Spirit here on earth whether to take away sickness from us, or to restore us to health when sickness has taken hold upon us.

Divine healing accompanies the sanctification by the Spirit. It is to make us holy that the Holy Spirit makes us partakers of Christ's redemption. Hence His name "Holy." Therefore the healing which He works is an intrinsic part of His divine mission, and He bestows it, whether to lead the sick one to be converted and to believe (Acts 4:29-30; 5:12, 14; 6:7-8; 8:6, 8; 9:42) or to confirm his faith if he is already converted. He constrains him thus to renounce sin, and to consecrate himself entirely to God and to His service (I Cor. 11:31; James 5:15-16; Heb. 12:10).

Divine healing tends to glorify Jesus. It is God's will that His Son should be glorified, and the Holy Spirit does this when He comes to show us what the redemption of Christ does for us. The redemption of the mortal body appears almost more marvelous than that of the immortal soul. In these two ways, God wills to dwell in us through Christ, and thus to triumph over the flesh. As soon as our body becomes the temple of God through the Spirit, Jesus is glorified.

Divine healing takes place wherever the Spirit of God works in power. Proofs of this are to be found in the lives of the Reformers, and in those of certain Moravians in their best times. But there are yet other promises touching the pouring out of the Holy Spirit which have not been fulfilled up to this time. Let us live in a holy expectation, praying the Lord to accomplish them in us.

Chapter 15

PERSEVERING PRAYER

(Luke 18:1-8)

The necessity of praying with perseverance is the secret of all spiritual life. What a blessing to be able to ask the Lord such and such a grace until He gives it, knowing with certainty that it is His will to answer prayer! But what a mystery for us is the call to persevere in prayer, to knock in faith at His door, to remind Him of His promises, and to do so without wearying until He arises and grants us our petition! Is not the assurance that our prayer should obtain from the Lord that which He would not otherwise give, the evident proof that man has been created in the image of God, that he is His friend, that he is His fellow-worker, and that the believers who together form the Body of Christ partake in this manner of His intercessory work? It is to Christ's intercession that the Father responds, and to which He grants His divine favors.

More than once the Bible explains to us the need for persevering prayer. There are many grounds, the chief of which is the justice of God. God has declared that sin must bear its consequences; sin, therefore, has rights over a world which welcomes and remains enslaved by it. When the child of God seeks to quit this order of things, it is necessary that the justice of God should consent to this; time, therefore, is needed that the privileges which Christ has procured for the believers should weigh before God's tribunal. Besides this, the opposition of Satan, who always seeks to prevent the answer to prayer, is a reason for it (Dan 10:12-13). The only means by which this unseen enemy can be conquered is faith. Standing firmly on the promises of God, faith refuses to yield, and continues to pray and wait for the answer, even when it is delayed, knowing that the victory is sure (Eph. 6:12-13).

Finally, perseverance in prayer is needful for ourselves. Delay in the answer is intended to prove and strengthen our faith; it ought to develop in us the steadfast will which will no longer let go the promises of God, but which renounces its own side of things to trust in God alone. It is then that God, seeing our faith, finds us ready to receive His favor and grants it to us. He will avenge speedily, even though He tarry. Yes, notwithstanding all the needful delays, He will not make us wait a moment too long. If we cry unto Him day and night, He will avenge us speedily.

This perseverance in prayer will become easy to us as soon as we fully understand what faith is. Jesus teaches us in these words: "All things whatsoever ye shall ask in prayer, believing, ye shall receive" (Matt. 21:22). When the Word of God authorizes us to ask anything, we ought at once to believe that we receive it. God gives it us; this we know by faith, and we can say between God and us that we have received it, although it might be only later that we are permitted to realize the effects here on earth. It is before having seen or experienced anything whatsoever that faith rejoices in having received, perseveres in praying and waiting until the answer is manifest. It is then precisely in order to count upon the answer that it is sometimes useful to continue to pray; and even after having believed that we are heard, it is good to persevere until it has become an accomplished fact.

This is of great importance in obtaining divine healing. Sometimes, it is true, that healing is immediate and complete; but it may happen that we have to wait, even when a sick person has been able to ask for healing in faith. Sometimes also, the first symptoms of healing are immediately manifest, but afterward, the progress is slow and interrupted by times when it is arrested or when the evil returns. In either case, it is important as much for the sick person as for those who pray with him, to believe in the efficacy of persevering prayer, even though they may not understand the mystery of it. That which God appears at first to refuse, He grants later to the prayer of the Canaanitish woman, to the prayer of the "widow," to that of the friend who knocks at midnight (Matt. 15:22-28; Luke 18:3-8; 11:5-8). Without regarding either change or answer, the faith which is grounded on the Word of God, and which continues to pray with importunity, ends by gaining the victory. "Shall not God avenge his own elect which cry day and night unto him, though he bear long with them? I tell you that he will avenge them speedily" (Luke 18:7-8). God knows how to delay all the time which is necessary, and nevertheless to act speedily without waiting more than is needful. The same two things should belong to our faith. Let us lay hold, with a holy promptitude, of the grace which is promised us, as if we had already received it; let us await with untiring patience the answer which is slow to come. Such faith belongs to living in Him. It is in order to produce in us this faith that sickness is sent to us, and that the healing is granted to us, for such faith above all glorifies God.

Chapter 16

LET HIM THAT IS HEALED GLORIFY GOD

(Luke 18:43; Acts 3:8)

It is a prevalent idea that piety is easier in sickness than in health; that silence and suffering incline the soul to seek the Lord, and enter into communion with Him better than the distractions of active life; that, in fact, sickness throws us more upon God. For these reasons, sick people hesitate to ask for healing from the Lord; for they say to themselves, How can we know whether sickness may not be better for us than health? To think thus is to ignore that healing and its fruits are divine. Let us try to understand that if healing through ordinary means may at times run the risk of making God relax His hand, divine healing, on the contrary, binds us more closely to Him. Thus it comes to pass that in our day, as in the time of the early ministry of Jesus Christ, the believer who has been healed by Him can glorify Him far better than the one who remains sick. Sickness can glorify God only in the measure in which it gives occasion to manifest His power (John 9:3; 11:4).

The sufferer who is led by his sufferings to give glory to God, does it, so to speak, by constraint. If he had health and the liberty to choose, it is quite possible that his heart would turn back to the world. In such a case, the Lord must keep him on one side; his piety depends on his sickly condition. This is why the world supposes that religion is hardly efficacious anywhere but in sick chambers or deathbeds, and for such as have no need to enter into the noise and stir of ordinary life. In order that the world may be convinced of the power of religion against temptation, it must see the believer who is in good health walking in calmness and holiness even in the midst of work and of active life. Doubtless very many sick people have glorified God by their patience in suffering, but He can be still more glorified by a health which He has sanctified.

Why then, we are asked, should those who have been healed in answer to the prayer of faith glorify the Lord more than such as have been healed through earthly remedies? Here is the reason. Healing by means of remedies shows us the power of God in nature, but it does not bring us into living and direct contact with Him; while divine healing is an act proceeding from God, without anything but the Holy Spirit.

In this latter, contact with God is the thing which is essential, and it is for this reason that examination of the conscience and the confession of sins should be the preparation for it (I Cor. 11:30-32; James 5: 15-16). One who is so healed is called to consecrate himself quite anew and entirely to the Lord (I Cor. 6:13, 19). All this depends upon the act of faith which lays hold of the Lord's promise, which yields to Him, and which does not doubt that the Lord at once takes possession of what is consecrated to Him. This is why the continuance of health received depends on the holiness of the life, and the obedience in seeking always the good pleasure of the divine Healer (Exod. 15:26).

Health obtained under such conditions ensures spiritual blessings much greater than the mere restoration to health by ordinary means. When the Lord heals the body, it is that He may take possession of it and make it a temple that He may dwell in. The joy which then fills the soul is indescribable; it is not only the joy of being healed, it is joy mingled with humility, and a holy enthusiasm which realizes the touch of the Lord, and which receives a new life from Him. In the exuberance of his joy, the healed one exalts the Lord, he glorifies Him by word and deed, and all his life is consecrated to his God.

It is evident that these fruits of healing are not the same for all, and that sometimes there are steps made backward. The life of the healed one has a solidarity with the life of believers around him. Their doubts and their inconsistencies may in time tend to make his steps totter, although this generally results in a new beginning. Each day he discovers and recognizes afresh that his life is the Lord's life; he enters into a more intimate and more joyous communion with Him; he learns to live in habitual dependence upon Jesus, and receives from Him that strength which results from a more complete consecration.

Oh, what may not the Church become when she lives in this faith, when every sick person shall recognize in sickness a call to be holy, and to expect from the Lord a manifestation of His presence, when healings shall be multiplied, producing in each a witness of the power of God, all ready to cry with the Psalm-ist, "Bless the Lord, O my soul . . . who healeth all thy diseases" (Ps. 103:2-3).

Chapter 17

THE NEED OF A MANIFESTATION OF GOD'S POWER

(Acts 4:29-31)

Is.it permissible to pray in this way now, to ask the Lord,. "Grant thy servants to speak thy word with all boldness while thou stretchest out thy hand to heal" (RV)? Let us look into this question.

Does not the Word of God meet with as many difficulties in our days as then, and are not the needs now equally pressing? Let us picture to ourselves the apostles in the midst of Jerusalem and her unbelief; on the one hand, the rulers of the people and their threatenings; on the other, the blinded multitude refusing to believe in the Crucified. Now the world is no longer so openly hostile to the Church because it has lost its fear of her, but its flattering words are more to be dreaded than its hatred. Dissimulation is sometimes worse than violence. Is not a Christianity of mere form, in the sleep of indifference, equally inaccessible with an openly resisting Judaism? God's servants need, even in the present day, in order that the Word may be preached with all boldness, that the power of God should be evidently manifested among them.

Is not the help of God as necessary now as then? The apostles knew well that it was not the eloquence of their preaching which caused the truth to triumph, but they knew then the need that the Holy Spirit should manifest His presence by miracles. It was needful that the living God should stretch forth His hand, that there might be healings, miracles, and signs in the name of His holy Son Jesus. It was only thus that His servants rejoiced, and, strengthened by His presence, could speak His Word with boldness and teach the world to fear His name.

Do not the divine promises concern us also? The apostles counted on these words of the Lord before He ascended: "Go ye into all the world, and preach the Gospel to every creature.... And these signs shall follow them that believe . . . they shall lay hands on the sick, and they shall recover" (Mark 16:15, 17-18). This charge indicates the divine vocation of the Church; the promise which follows it shows us what is her armor, and proves to us that the Lord acts in concert with her. It was because the apostles counted on this promise that they prayed the Lord to grant them this proof of His presence. They had been filled with the Holy Ghost on the Day of Pentecost, but they still needed the supernatural signs which His power works. The same promise is as much for us, for the command to preach the Gospel cannot be severed from the promise of divine healing with which it is accompanied. It is nowhere to be found in the Bible that this promise was not for future times. In all ages, God's people greatly need to know that the Lord is with them, and to possess the irrefutable proof of it. Therefore, this promise is for us; let us pray for its fulfilment.

Ought we to reckon on the same grace? We read in the Acts that when the apostles had prayed, "they were all filled with the Holy Ghost, and they spake the word of God with boldness. . . . And by the hands of the apostles were many signs and wonders wrought among the people . . . and believers were the more added to the Lord, multitudes both of men and women" (Acts 4:31; 5:12, 14). Oh, what joy and what new strength would God's people receive today if anew the Lord should thus stretch forth His hand! How many wearied and discouraged laborers grieve that they do not see more result, more blessing on their labors! What life would come into their faith if signs of this kind should arise to prove to them that God is with them! Many who are indifferent would be led to reflect, more than one doubter would regain confidence, and all unbelievers would be reduced to silence. And the poor heathen! How he would awake if he saw by facts that which words had not enabled him to lay hold of, if he were forced to acknowledge that the Christian's God is the living God who does wonders, the God of love who blesses!

Awake, awake, put on your strength, Church of Christ. Although you have lost by your unfaithfulness the joy of seeing allied to the preaching of the Word the hand of the Lord stretched out to heal, the Lord is ready to grant you this grace again. Acknowledge that it is thine own unbelief which has so long deprived you of it, and pray for pardon. Clothe yourself with the strength of prayer.

"*Awake, awake, put on strength, O arm of the Lord. Awake as in the ancient days*" *(Isa. 51:9).*

Chapter 18

SIN AND SICKNESS

The prayer of faith shall save the sick, and the Lord shall raise him up; and if he have committed sins, they shall be forgiven him. Confess your faults one to another, and pray one for another, that ye may be healed. (James 5:15-16)

Here, as in other Scriptures, the pardon of sins and the healing of sickness are closely united. James declares that pardon of sins will be granted with the healing; and for this reason, he desires to see confession of sin accompany the prayer which claims healing. We know that confession of sin is indispensable to obtain from God the pardon of sin; it is not less so to obtain healing. Unconfessed sin presents an obstacle to the prayer of faith; in any case, the sickness may soon reappear, and for this reason.

The first care of a physician, when he is called to treat a patient, is to diagnose the cause of the disease. If he succeeds, he stands a better chance to combat it. Our God also goes back to the primary cause of all sickness—that is sin. It is their part to confess, and God's to grant the pardon which removes this first cause, so that healing can take place. In seeking for healing by means of earthly remedies, the first thing to do is to find a clever physician, and then to follow his prescriptions exactly; but in having recourse to the prayer of faith, it is needful to fix our eyes, above all, upon the Lord, and to ascertain how we stand with Him. James, therefore, points out to us a condition which is essential to the recovery of our health; namely, that we confess and forsake sin.

Sickness is a consequence of sin. It is because of sin that God permits it; it is in order to show us our faults, to chasten us, and purify us from them. Sickness is therefore a visible sign of God's judgment upon sin. It is not that the one who is sick is necessarily a greater sinner than another who is in health. On the contrary, it is often the most holy among the children of God whom He chastens, as we see from the example of Job. Neither is it always to check some fault which we can easily determine; it is especially to draw the attention of the sick one to that which remains in him of the egotism of the "old man" and of all which hinders him from a life entirely consecrated to his God. The first step which the sick one has to take in the path of divine healing will be, therefore, to let the Holy Spirit of God probe his heart and convince him of sin, after which will come, also, humiliation, decision to break with sin, and confession. To confess our sins is to lay them down before God and to subject them to His judgment, with the fixed purpose to fall into them no more. A sincere confession will be followed by a new assurance of pardon.

"If he has committed sins, they shall be forgiven him." When we have confessed our sins, we must receive also the promised pardon, believing that God gives it. Faith in God's pardon is often vague in the child of God. Either he is uncertain, or he returns to old impressions, to the time when he first received pardon. But if the pardon which he now receives is with confidence, in answer to the prayer of faith, it will bring him new life and strength. The soul then rests under the efficacy of the blood of Christ, receives from the Holy Spirit the certainty of the pardon of sin, and therefore nothing remains to hinder the Savior from filling him with His love and with His grace. God's pardon brings with it a divine life which acts powerfully upon him who receives it.

When the soul has consented to make a sincere confession and has obtained pardon, it is ready to lay hold of the promise of God; it is no longer difficult to believe that the Lord will raise up His sick one. It is when we keep far from God that it is difficult to believe; confession and pardon bring us quite near to Him. As soon as the cause of the sickness has been removed, the sickness itself can be arrested. Now it is easy for the sick one to believe that if the Lord necessarily subjected the body to the chastisement of the sins committed, He also wills that, the sin being pardoned, this same body should receive the grace which manifests His love. His presence is revealed, a ray of life—of His divine life—comes to quicken the body, and the sick one proves that as soon as he is no longer separated from the Lord, the prayer of faith does save the sick.

Chapter 19

JESUS BORE OUR SICKNESS

He has borne our sicknesses and carried our pains. . . . My righteous servant [shall] justify many, for he shall bear their iniquities. . . . He shall divide the spoil with the strong, because . . . he bare the sin of many. (Isa. 53:4 RSV, margin, 11-12)

Do you know the beautiful fifty-third chapter of Isaiah, which has been called the fifth Gospel? In the light of the Spirit of God, Isaiah describes beforehand the sufferings of the Lamb of God, as well as the divine graces which should result from them.
should result from them.

The expression, "to bear," could not but appear in this prophecy. It is, in fact, the word which must accompany the mention of sin, whether as committed directly by the sinner, or whether as transmitted to a substitute. The transgressor, the priest, and the expiatory victim must all bear the sin. In the same way, it is because the Lamb of God has borne our sins, that God smote Him for the iniquity of us all. Sin was not found in Him, but it was put upon Him; He took it voluntarily upon Him. And it is because He bore it, and in bearing it, He put an end to it, that He has the power to save us. "My righteous servant shall justify many, for he shall bear their iniquities . . . he shall divide the spoil with the strong, because . . . he bare the sin of many" (Isa. 53:11-12). It is, therefore, because our sins have been borne by Jesus Christ, that we are delivered from them as soon as we believe this truth; consequently, we have no longer to bear them ourselves.

In this chapter, the expression "to bear" occurs twice, but in relation to two different things. It is not said only that the Lord's righteous Servant had borne the sins (v. 12), but also that He has borne our sickness (v. 4 RV, margin). Thus His bearing our sicknesses as well as our sins forms an integral part of the Redeemer's work. Although Himself without sin, He has borne our sins, and He has done as much for our sicknesses. The human nature of Jesus could not be touched by sickness, because it remained holy. We never find in the account of His life any mention of sickness. Participating in all the weaknesses of our human nature, hunger, thirst, fatigue, and sleep, because these things are not the consequence of sin, He still had no trace of sickness. As He was without sin, sickness had no hold on Him, and He could die only a violent death, and that by His voluntary consent. Thus it is not in Him but on Him that we see sickness as well as sin; He took them upon Him and bore them of His own free will. In bearing them and taking them upon Him, He has, by the very fact, triumphed over them, and has acquired the right of delivering His children from them.

Sin had attacked and ruined equally the soul and the body. Jesus came to save both. Having taken upon Him sickness as well as sin, He is in a position to set us free from the one as well as the other, and that He may accomplish this double deliverance, He expects from us only one thing: our faith.

As soon as a sick believer understands the meaning of the words, "Jesus has borne my sins," he does not fear to say also, "I need no longer bear my sins; they are upon me no longer." In the same way, as soon as he has fully taken in and believed for himself that Jesus has borne our sicknesses, he does not fear to say, "I need no longer bear my sickness; Jesus, in bearing sin, bore also sickness, which is its consequence; for both He has made propitiation, and He delivers me from both."

I myself witnessed the blessed influence which this truth exercised one day upon a sick woman. For seven years she had almost entirely kept her bed. A sufferer from tuberculosis, epilepsy, and other sicknesses, she had been assured that no hope of cure remained for her. She was carried into the room where the late Mr. W. E. Boardman was holding a Sunday evening service for the sick, and was laid in a half-fainting condition on the sofa. She was too little conscious to remember anything of what took place until she heard the words, "Himself took our infirmities and bare our sicknesses" (Matt. 8:17), and then she seemed to hear the words, "If He has borne your sicknesses, why then bear them yourself? Get up."

"But," she thought, "if I attempt to get up, and fall upon the ground, what will they think of me?"

But the inward voice began again, "If He has borne my sins, why should I have to bear them?" To the astonishment of all who were present, she arose, and, although still feeble, sat down in a chair by the table. From that moment, her healing made rapid progress.

At the end of a few weeks, she had no longer the appearance of an invalid, and later on, her strength was such that she could spend many hours a day in visiting the poor. With what joy and love she could then speak of Him who was "the strength of her life" (Ps. 27:1). She had believed that Jesus had borne her sicknesses as well as her sins, and her faith was not put to confusion. It is thus that Jesus reveals Himself as a perfect Savior to all those who will trust themselves unreservedly to Him.

Chapter 20

IS SICKNESS A CHASTISEMENT?

For this cause many among you are weak and sickly, and not a few sleep. For if we discerned ourselves, we should not be judged. But when we are judged, we are chastened of the Lord, that we may not be condemned with the world. (I Cor. 11:30-32 RV)

In writing to the Corinthians, the apostle Paul had to reprove them for the manner in which they observed the Lord's Supper, drawing upon themselves the chastisement of God. Here, therefore, we see sickness as a judgment of God, a chastisement for sin. Paul sees it to be a real chastisement, since he afterward says, "chastened by the Lord," and he adds that it is in order to hinder them from falling yet deeper into sin, to prevent them from being "condemned with the world" that they are thus afflicted. He warns them that if they would be neither judged nor chastened by the Lord, that if by such examination they discovered the cause of the sickness and condemned their sins, the Lord would no longer need to exercise severity. Is it not evident that here sickness is a judgment of God, a chastisement of sin, and that we may avoid it by examining and condemning ourselves?

Yes, sickness is, more often than we believe it, a judgment, a chastisement for sin. God "doth not afflict willingly nor grieve the children of men" (Lam. 3:33). It is not without a cause that He deprives us of health. Perhaps it may be to render us attentive to some sin which we can recognize; "Sin no more, lest a worse thing come unto thee" (John 5:14); perhaps because God's child has got entangled in pride and worldliness; or it may be that self-confidence or caprice have been mixed with one's service for God. It is again quite possible that the chastisement may not be directed against any particular sin, but that it may be the result of the preponderance of sin which weighs upon the entire human race. When in the case of the man born blind, the disciples asked the Lord, "Who did sin, this man or his parents, that he was born blind?" and He answered, "Neither hath this man sinned nor his parents" (John 9:3), He does not by any means say that there is no relation between sin and sickness, but

He teaches us not to accuse every sick person of sin.

In any case, sickness is always a discipline which ought to awaken our attention to sin, and turn us from it. Therefore a sick person should begin by condemning, or discerning himself (I Cor. 11:31), by placing himself before his heavenly Father with a sincere desire to see anything which could have grieved Him, or could have rendered the chastisement necessary. In so doing, he may count assuredly on the Holy Spirit's light, who will clearly show him his failure. Let him be ready at once to renounce what he may discern, and to place himself at the Lord's disposal to serve Him with perfect obedience, but let him not imagine that he can conquer sin by his own efforts. No, that is impossible to him. But let him, with all his power of will, be on God's side in renouncing what is sin in His sight, and let him believe that he is accepted of Him. In so doing, he will be yielding himself, consecrating himself anew to God, willing to do only His holy will in all things.

Scripture assures us that if we thus examine ourselves, the Lord will not judge us. Our Father chastens His child only as far as is needful. God seeks to deliver us from sin and self. As soon as we understand Him and break with these, sickness may cease; it has done its work. We must come to see what the sickness means, and recognize in it the discipline of God. One may recognize vaguely that he commits sins, while scarcely attempting to define what they are; or if he does, he may not believe it is possible to give them up; and if he decides to renounce them, he may fail to count on God that He will put an end to the chastisement. And yet, how glorious is the assurance which Paul's words here give us!

Dear sick one, do you understand that your heavenly Father has something to reprove in you? He would have your sickness help you to discover it, and the Holy Spirit will guide you in the search. Then renounce at once what He may point out to you. You would not have the smallest shade remain between your Father and you. It is His will to pardon your sin and to heal your sickness. In Jesus we have both pardon and healing; they are two sides of His redemptive work. He calls you to live a life of dependence upon Him in a greater degree than hitherto. Abandon yourself then to Him in a complete obedience, and walk henceforth as a little child in following His steps. It is with joy that your heavenly Father will deliver you from chastisement, that He will reveal Himself to you as your Healer, that He will bring you nearer to Him by this new tie of His love, that He will make you obedient and faithful in serving Him. If, as a wise and faithful Father, He has been obliged to chasten you, it is also as a Father that He wills your healing, and that He desires to bless and keep you henceforth.

Chapter 21

GOD'S PRESCRIPTION
FOR THE SICK

Is any sick among you? Let him call for the elders of the
church, and let them pray over him, anointing him with oil in
the name of the Lord; and the prayer of faith shall save the
sick, and the Lord shall raise him up, and if he have committed
sins, they shall be forgiven him. (James 5:14-15)

James 5:14-15, above all other Scriptures,
is that which most clearly declares to the sick
what they have to do in order to be healed.
Sickness and its consequences abound in the
world. What joy, then, for the believer to
learn from the Word of God the way of healing for the sick! The Bible teaches us that it is
the will of God to see His children in good
health. The apostle James has no hesitation
in saying that "the prayer of faith shall save
the sick, and the Lord shall raise him up."
May the Lord teach us to hearken and to re-

ceive with simplicity what His Word tells us!

Notice, first, that James here makes a distinction between affliction (or suffering) and sickness. He says, "Is any among you afflicted? let him pray" (v. 13). He does not specify what shall be requested in such a case; still less does he say that deliverance from suffering shall be asked. No; suffering which may arise from various exterior causes is the portion of every Christian. Let us therefore understand that the object of James is to lead the tried believer to ask for deliverance only with a spirit of submission to the will of God, and, above all, to ask the patience which he considers to be the privilege of the believer (James 1:2-4, 12; 5:7-8).

But in dealing with the words, "Is any sick among you?" James replies in quite another manner. He says with assurance that the sick one may ask for healing with confidence that he shall obtain it, and the Lord will hear him. There is, therefore, a great difference between suffering and sickness. The Lord Jesus spoke of suffering as being necessary, as being willed and blessed of God, while He says of sickness that it ought to be cured. All other suffering comes to us from without, and will cease only when Jesus shall triumph over the sin and evil which are in the world. Sickness is an evil which is in the body itself, in this body saved by Christ that it may become the temple of the Holy Spirit, and which, consequently, ought to be healed as soon as the sick believer receives by faith the working of the Holy Spirit, the very life of Jesus in him.

What is the direction here given to the sick? Let him call for the elders of the church, and let the elders pray for him. In the time of James, there were physicians, but it is not to them that the sick believer must turn. The elders then were the pastors and leaders of the churches, called to the ministry not because they had passed through schools of theology, but because they were filled with the Holy Spirit, and well known for their piety and for their faith. Why should their presence be needed by the sick one? Could he not have prayed for himself? Could not his friends have prayed? Yes, but it is not so easy for everybody to exercise the faith which obtains healing, and, doubtless, that is one reason why James desired that men should be called whose faith was firm and sure. Besides this, they were representatives to the sick one of the Church, the collective Body of Christ, for it is the communion of believers which invites the Spirit to act with power. In short, they should, after the pattern of the great

Shepherd of the sheep, care for the flock as He does, identify themselves with the sick one, understand his trouble, receive from God the necessary discernment to instruct him and encourage him to persevere in faith. It is, then, to the elders of the Church that the healing of the sick is committed, and it is they, the servants of the God who pardons iniquities and heals diseases (Ps. 103), who are called to transmit to others the Lord's graces for soul and body.

Finally, there is a promise still more direct—that of healing; the apostle speaks of it as the certain consequence of the prayer of faith. "The prayer of faith shall save the sick, and the Lord shall raise him up." This promise ought to stimulate in every believer the desire and expectation of healing. Receiving these words with simplicity and as they are written, ought we not to see in them an unlimited promise, offering healing to whosoever shall pray in faith? The Lord teach us to study His Word with the faith of a truly believing heart!

Chapter 22

THE LORD THAT HEALETH THEE

I will put none of these diseases upon thee which I have brought upon the Egyptians, for I am the Lord that healeth thee. (Exod. 15:26)

How often have we read these words, without daring to take them for ourselves, and without expectation that the Lord would fulfill them to us! We have seen in them that the people of God ought to be exempt from the diseases inflicted upon the Egyptians, and we have believed that this promise applied only to the Old Testament, and that we who live under the economy of the New Testament cannot expect to be kept from, or healed of, sickness by the direct intervention of the Lord! As, however, we were obliged to recognize the superiority of the New Covenant, we have come, in our ignorance, to allege that sickness often brings great blessings, and that consequently God had done well to withdraw what He had formerly promised, and to be no longer for us what He was for Israel, "the Lord that healeth thee."

But in our day, we see the Church awakening and acknowledging her mistake. She sees that it is under the New Covenant that the Lord Jesus acquired the title of Healer by all His miraculous healings. She is beginning to see that in charging His Church to preach the Gospel to every creature, He has promised to be with her "alway, even unto the end of the world" (Matt. 28:20), and as the proof of His presence, His disciples should have the power to lay hands on the sick, and they should be healed (Mark 16:15-18). She sees, moreover, that in the days of Pentecost, the miraculous pouring out of the Holy Spirit was accompanied by miraculous healings, which were evident proof of the blessings brought about by the power from on high (Acts 3:16; 5:12; 9:40). There is nothing in the Bible to make her believe that the promise made to Israel has been since retracted, and she hears from the mouth of the apostle James this new promise: "The prayer of faith shall save (or heal) the sick" (James 5:15). She knows that at all times it has been unbelief which has limited (or set bounds to) the Holy One of

Israel (Ps. 78:41), and she asks herself if it is not unbelief which hinders in these days this manifestation of the power of God. Who can doubt it? It is not God or His Word which are to blame here; it is our unbelief which prevents the miraculous power of the Lord, and which holds Him back from healing as in past times. Let our faith awake, let it recognize and adore in Christ the all-power of Him who says, "I am the Lord which healeth thee." It is by the works of God that we can best understand what His Word tells us; the healings which again are responding to the prayer of faith confirm, by gloriously illustrating, the truth of His promise.

Let us learn to see in the risen Jesus the divine Healer, and let us receive Him as such. In order that I may recognize in Jesus my justification, my strength, and my wisdom, I must grasp by faith that He is really all this to me; and equally when the Bible tells me that Jesus is the sovereign Healer, I must myself appropriate this truth, and say, "Yes, Lord, it is Thou who art my Healer." And why may I hold Him as such? It is because He gives Himself to me, that I am "one plant with him" (Rom. 6:5 French ver.), and that, inseparably united to Him, I thus possess His healing power; it is because His love is pleased to load His beloved with His favors, to communicate Himself with all His heart to all who desire to receive Him. Let us believe that He is ready to extend the treasure of blessing, contained in the name, "The Lord that healeth thee," to all who know and who can trust in this divine name. This is the treatment for the sick indicated by the law of His kingdom.

When I bring my sickness to the Lord, I do not depend on what I see, on what I feel, or what I think, but on what He says. Even when everything appears contrary to the expected healing, even if it should not take place at the time or in the way that I had thought I should receive it, even when the symptoms seem only to be aggravated, my faith, strengthened by the very waiting, should cling immovably to this word which has gone out of the mouth of God, "I am the Lord that healeth thee." God is ever seeking to make us true believers. Healing and health are of little value if they do not glorify God, and serve to unite us more closely with Him; thus in the matter of healing, our faith must always be put to the proof. He who counts on the name of his God, who can hear Jesus saying to him, "Said I not unto thee that if thou wouldest believe thou shouldest see the glory of God?" (John 11:

40), will have the joy of receiving from God Himself the healing of the body, and of seeing it take place in a manner worthy of God, and conformably to His promises. When we read these words, "I am the Lord that healeth thee," let us not fear to answer eagerly, "Yes, Lord, Thou art the Lord that healeth me."

Chapter 23

JESUS HEALS THE SICK

He . . . healed all that were sick that it might be fulfilled
which was spoken by Esaias the prophet, saying: Himself took
our infirmities and bare our sicknesses. (Matt: 8:16-17)

In a preceding chapter, we have studied
the words of the prophet Isaiah. If the reader
has still any doubt as to the interpretation
which has been given, we remind him of that
which the Holy Spirit caused the evangelist
St. Matthew to write. It is expressly said regarding all the sick ones whom Jesus healed,
"That it might be fulfilled which was spoken
by Esaias the prophet." It was because Jesus
had taken on Him our sicknesses that He
could, that He ought to heal them. If He had
not done so, one part of His work of redemption would have remained powerless and
fruitless.

This text of the Word of God is not generally understood in this way. It is the generally accepted view that the miraculous healings done by the Lord Jesus are to be looked upon only as the proof of His mercy, or as being the symbol of spiritual graces. They are not seen to be a necessary consequence of redemption, although that is what the Bible declares. The body and the soul have been created to serve together as a habitation of God; the sickly condition of the body, as well as that of the soul, is a consequence of sin, and that is what Jesus came to bear, to expiate, and to conquer.

When the Lord Jesus was on earth, it was not in the character of the Son of God that He cured the sick, but as the Mediator who had taken upon Him and borne sickness, and this enables us to understand why Jesus gave so much time to His healing work, and why also the evangelists speak of it in a manner so detailed. Read for example what Matthew says about it: "Jesus went about all Galilee, teaching in their synagogues, and preaching the gospel of the kingdom, and healing all manner of sickness, and all manner of disease among the people. And his fame went throughout all Syria; and they brought unto him all sick people that were taken with divers diseases and torments, and those which were possessed with devils, and those which were lunatic, and those that had the palsy; and he healed them" (4:23-24). "And Jesus went about all the cities and villages, teaching in their synagogues and preaching the Gospel of the kingdom, and healing every sickness and every disease among the people" (9:35). "And when he had called unto him his twelve disciples, he gave them power against unclean spirits, to cast them out, and to heal all manner of sickness, and all manner of disease" (10:1).

When the disciples of John the Baptist came to ask Jesus if He were the Messiah, that He might prove it to them, He replied, "The blind receive their sight, and the lame walk, the lepers are cleansed, and the deaf hear, the dead are raised up, and the poor have the gospel preached to them" (11:5). After the cure of the withered hand, and the opposition of the Pharisees who sought to destroy Him, we read that "great multitudes followed him, and he healed them all" (12: 15). When later, the multitude had followed Him into a desert place, it is said, "And Jesus went forth and saw a great multitude, and was moved with compassion toward them, and he healed their sick" (14:14). Farther on, "They sent out into all that country round about, and brought unto him all that were diseased; and besought him that they might only touch the hem of his garment; and as many as touched were made perfectly whole" (14:35-36). It is said also of the sick which were among the multitudes that they "cast them down at Jesus' feet and he healed them," and Matthew adds, "insomuch that the multitude wondered when they saw the dumb to speak, the maimed to be whole, the lame to walk, and the blind to see, and they glorified the God of Israel" (15:30-31). And finally, when He came into the coasts of Judea beyond Jordan, "Great multitudes followed him, and he healed them there" (19:2).

Let us add to these divers texts those which give us in detail the account of healings wrought by Jesus, and let us ask ourselves if these healings afford us only the proof of His power during His life here on earth, or if they are not much rather the undoubted and continual result of His work of mercy and of love, the manifestation of His power of redemption which delivers the soul and body from the dominion of sin? Yes; that was in very deed the purpose of God. If, then, Jesus bore our sicknesses as an integral part of the redemption, if He has healed the sick "that it might be fulfilled which was spoken by Esaias," and if His Savior-heart is always full of mercy and of love, we can believe with certainty that to this very day it is the will of Jesus to heal the sick in answer to the prayer of faith.

Chapter 24

FERVENT AND
EFFECTUAL PRAYER

Pray one for another that ye may be healed. The effectual, fervent prayer of a righteous man availeth much. Elijah was a man of like passions (or nature) with us and he prayed fervently that it might not rain, and it rained not on the earth for three years and six months. And he prayed again; and the heaven gave rain, and the earth brought forth her fruit. (James 5:16 KJV, 17-18 ASV)

James knew that a faith which obtains healing is not the fruit of human nature; therefore he adds that the prayer must be "fervent." Only such prayer can be efficacious. In this he stands upon the example of Elijah, a man of the same nature ("subject to like passions") as we are, drawing therefore the inference that our prayer can be and ought to be of the same nature as his. How then did Elijah pray? This will throw some light upon what the prayer of faith should be.

Elijah had received from God the promise that rain was about to fall upon the earth (I Kings 18:1), and he had declared this to Ahab. Strong in the promise of his God, he mounts Carmel to pray (I Kings 18:42; James 5:18). He knows, he believes, that God's will is to send rain, and nevertheless he must pray, or the rain will not come. His prayer is no empty form; it is a real power, the efficacy of which is about to make itself felt in heaven. God wills that it shall rain, but the rain will come only at Elijah's request, a request repeated with faith and perseverance until the appearance of the first cloud in the sky. In order that the will of God shall be accomplished, this will must on one side be expressed by a promise, and on the other it must be received and laid hold of by the believer who prays. He therefore must persevere in prayer that he may show his God that his faith expects an answer, and will not grow weary until it is obtained.

This is how prayer must be made for the sick. The promise of God, "The Lord will raise him up," must be rested on, and His will to heal recognized. Jesus Himself teaches us to pray with faith which counts on the answer of God. He says to us, "All things whatsoever ye pray for, and ask for, believe that ye have received them and ye shall have them" (Mark 11:24 RV). After the prayer of faith which receives beforehand that which God has promised, comes the prayer of perseverance, which does not lose sight of that which has been asked until God has fulfilled His promise (I Kings 18:43). There may be some obstacle which hinders the fulfilment of the promise; whether on the side of God and His righteousness (Deut. 9:18), or on the side of Satan, and his constant opposition to the plans of God, something which may still impede the answer to the prayer (Dan. 10:12-13). It may be also that our faith needs to be purified (Matt. 15: 22-28). Whatever it may be, our faith is called to persevere until the answer comes. He who prays six times fervently and stops there, when he ought to have prayed seven times (II Kings 13:18-19), deprives himself of the answer to his prayer.

Perseverance in prayer, a perseverance which strengthens the faith of the believer against all which may seem opposed to the answer, is a real miracle; it is one of the impenetrable mysteries of the life of faith. Does it not say to us the Savior's redeemed one is in very deed His friend, a member of His body, and that the government of the world and the gifts of divine grace depend in some sense upon his prayers? Prayer, therefore, is no vain form. It is the work of the Holy Spirit, who intercedes here on earth in us and by us, and as such, it is as efficacious, as indispensable as the work of the Son interceding for us before the throne of God. It might seem strange that after having prayed with the certainty of being heard, and having seen therein the will of God, we should still need to continue in prayer. Nevertheless, it is so. In Gethsemane, Jesus prayed three times in succession. On Carmel, Elijah prayed seven times; and we, if we believe the promise of God without doubting, shall pray until we receive the answer. Both the importunate friend at midnight and the widow who besieged the unjust judge are examples of perseverance in seeking the end in view.

Let us learn from Elijah's prayer to humble ourselves, to recognize why the power of God cannot be more manifested in the Church, whether in the healing of the sick, or in conversion, or sanctification. "Ye have not because ye ask not" (James 4:2). Let it also teach us patience. In the cases where healing is delayed, let us remember that obstacles may exist over which only perseverance in prayer can triumph. Faith which ceases to pray, or which is allowed to relax in its fervor, cannot appropriate that which God has nevertheless given. Let not our faith in the promises of Scripture be shaken by those things which are as yet beyond our reach. God's promise remains the same: "The prayer of faith shall save the sick." May the prayer of Elijah strengthen our faith. Let us remember that we have to imitate them who through faith and patience inherit the promises (Heb. 6:12). If we learn to persevere in prayer, its fruit will be always more abundant, always more evident, and we shall obtain, as Jesus obtained when He was on earth, healing of the sick, often immediate healing, which shall bring glory to God.

Chapter 25

INTERCESSORY PRAYER

Confess therefore your sins one to another, and pray one for another that ye may be healed. The supplication of a righteous man availeth much in its working. (James 5:16 ASV)

James begins by speaking to us of the prayers of the elders of the church; but here he addresses all believers in saying, "Pray one for another that ye may be healed." Having already spoken of confession and of pardon, he still adds, "Confess your sins one to another."

This shows us that the prayer of faith which asks for healing is not the prayer of one isolated believer, but that it ought to unite the members of the Body of Christ in the communion of the Spirit. God certainly hears the prayer of each one of His children as soon as it is presented to Him with living faith, but the sick one does not always possess such faith as this; and that the Holy Spirit may come to act with power, there must be the union of several members of the Body of Christ unitedly claiming His presence. We need one as well as the other.

This dependence on our brethren should be exercised in two ways. First of all, we must confess our faults to any whom we may have wronged, and receive pardon from them. But besides this, if one who is sick has been brought to see in such or such a sin which he has committed the cause of his sickness, and to recognize in it a chastening of God, he ought in such a case to acknowledge his sin before the elders, or brethren in Christ who pray for him, and who are thus enabled to do so with more light and more faith. Such confession will be also a touchstone which tests the sincerity of his repentance, for it is easier to confess our sins to God than to man. Before a man confesses, his humiliation needs to be real and his repentance sincere. The result will be a closer communion between the sick one and those who intercede for him, and their faith will be quickened anew.

"Pray one for another that ye may be healed." Does not this clearly answer that which one so often hears said: What is the use in going to miracle-working evangelists in faraway places? Does not the Lord hear prayer in whatsoever place it is offered? Yes, without any doubt, wherever a prayer in living faith rises up to God, it finds Him ready to grant healing; but the Church has so neglected to believe in this truth, that it is a rare thing in the present day to find Christians capable of praying in this manner. Thus we cannot be too grateful to the Lord that He has inspired certain believers with the desire to consecrate their lives, in part, to witness to the truth of divine healing. Their words and their faith awaken faith in the heart of many sick ones who, without their help, would never arrive at it. It is precisely these very people who always say to everybody, "The Lord is everywhere to be found." Let Christians learn not to neglect the least part of the marvelous power of their God, and He will be able to manifest to all that He is always "the Lord which healeth thee" (Exod. 15:26). Let us take heed to obey the Word of God, to confess one to another and to pray one for another that we may be healed.

James notes here still another essential condition to successful prayer: it must be the prayer of the righteous. "The supplication of a righteous man availeth much in its working." The Scripture tells us that "he that doeth righteousness is righteous, even as he (Jesus) is righteous" (I John 3:7). James himself was surnamed "The Just," on account of his piety and the tenderness of his conscience. Whether an "elder" or a simple believer, it is only after one is wholly surrendered to God and living in obedience to His will, that one can pray effectually for the brethren. John says as much: "Whatsoever we ask, we receive of him, because we keep his commandments, and do those things which are pleasing in his sight" (I John 3:22). It is therefore the prayer of one who lives in intimate communion with God which "availeth much." It is to such prayer that God will grant the answer which He would not be able to give to some others of His children who do not live as close to Him.

We often hear these words quoted: "The prayer of a righteous man availeth much," but very rarely is it taken in connection with its context, or remembered that it is divine healing in particular which is in question here. Oh, may the Lord raise up in His Church many of these righteous men, animated with living faith, whom He can use to glorify Jesus as the divine Healer of the sick!

Chapter 26

THE WILL OF GOD

Thy will be done. (Matt. 6:10)
If the Lord will. (James 4:15)

In days of sickness, when doctors and medicines fail, recourse is generally had to such Scriptures as, "Thy will be done"(Matt. 6:10), and "If the Lord will" (James 4:15), and they may easily become a stumbling block in the way of divine healing. How may I know, it is asked, whether it is not God's will that I should remain ill? And as long as this is an open question, how can I believe for healing, how can I pray for it with faith? Here truth and error seem to touch. It is indeed impossible to pray with faith when we are not sure that we are asking according to the will of God. "I can," one may say, "pray fervently in asking God to do the best for me, believing that He will cure me if it is possible." As long as one prays thus, one is indeed praying with submission, but this is not the prayer of faith. That is only possible when we are certain that we are asking according to the will of God. The question then resolves itself into how we can know what is the will of God. It is a great mistake to think that the child of God cannot know His will about healing.

In order to know His divine will, we must be guided by the Word of God. It is His Word which promises us healing. The promise of James 5 is so absolute that it is impossible to deny it. This promise only confirms other passages, equally strong, which tell us that Jesus Christ has obtained for us the healing of our diseases, because He has borne our sicknesses. According to this promise, we have right to healing, because it is a part of the salvation which we have in Christ, and therefore we may expect it with certainty. Scripture tells us that sickness is, in God's hands, the means of chastening His children for their sins, but that this discipline ceases to be exercised as soon as His suffering child acknowledges and turns from the sin. Is it not as much as to say clearly that God desires to make use of sickness only to bring back His children when they are straying?

Sick Christian, open your Bible, study it,

and see in its pages that sickness is a warning to renounce sin, but that whoever acknowledges and forsakes his sins finds in Jesus pardon and healing. Such is God's promise in His Word. If the Lord had in view some other dispensation for such of His children whom He was about to call home to Him, He would make known to them His will, giving them by the Holy Spirit a desire to depart. In other special cases, He would awaken some special conviction; but as a general rule, the Word of God promises us healing in answer to the prayer of faith.

"Nevertheless," some might say, "is it not better in all things to leave it to the will of God?" And they quote the instance of such and such Christians who would have, so to speak, forced the hand of God by their praying without adding, "Thy will be done," and who would not have experienced blessing in the answer to their prayers. And these would say, "How do we know whether sickness would not be better for us than health?" Notice here that this is no case of forcing the hand of God, since it is His Word which tells us that it is His will to heal us. "The prayer of faith shall save the sick." God wills that the health of the soul should have a blessed reflex influence on the health of the body, that the presence of Jesus in the soul should have its confirmation in the good condition of the body. And when you know that such is His will, you cannot, when speaking in such a way, say truthfully that you are in all things leaving it to Him. It is not leaving it to Him when you make use of all possible remedies to get healing, instead of laying hold of His promise. Your submission is nothing else than spiritual sloth in view of that which God commands you to do.

As to knowing whether sickness is not better than health, we do not hesitate to reply that the return to health which is the fruit of giving up sin, of consecration to God, and of an ultimate communion with God, is infinitely better than sickness. "This is the will of God, even your sanctification" (I Thess. 4:3), and it is by healing that God confirms the reality of this. When Jesus comes to take possession of our body, and cures it miraculously, when it follows that the health received must be maintained from day to day by an uninterrupted communion with Him, the experience which we thus make of the Savior's power and of His love is a result very superior to any which sickness has to offer. Doubtless sickness may teach us submission, but healing received direct from God makes us better acquainted with our Lord, and teaches us to confide in Him better. Besides which, it prepares the believer to accomplish better the service of God.

Sick Christian, if you would really seek to know what is the will of God in this thing, do not let yourself be influenced by the opinions of others, nor by your own former prejudices, but listen to and study what the Word of God has to say. Examine whether it does not tell you that divine healing is a part of the redemption of Jesus, and that God wills that every believer should have the right to claim it. See whether it does not promise that the prayer of every child of God for this thing shall be heard, and whether health restored by the power of the Holy Spirit does not manifest the glory of God in the eyes of the Church and of the world. Inquire of it; it will answer you, that, according to the will of God, sickness is a discipline occasioned by sin (or shortcoming), and that healing, granted to the prayer of faith, bears witness to His grace which pardons, which sanctifies, and which takes away sin.

Chapter 27
OBEDIENCE AND HEALTH

There he made for them a statute and an ordinance, and there he proved them, and said, If thou wilt diligently hearken to the voice of the Lord thy God, and wilt do that which is right in his sight, and wilt give ear to his commandments, and keep all his statutes, I will put none of these diseases upon thee which I have brought upon the Egyptians; for I am the Lord that healeth thee. (Exod. 15:25-26)

Israel was just released from the yoke of Egypt when their faith was put to the proof in the desert by the waters of Marah. It was after He had sweetened the bitter waters that the Lord promised He would not put upon the children of Israel any of the diseases which He had brought upon the Egyptians as long as they would obey Him. They would be exposed to other trials, they might sometimes suffer the need of bread and of water, they would have to contend with mighty foes, and encounter great dangers; all these things might come upon them in spite of their obedience, but sickness might not touch them. In a world still under the power of Satan, they might be a butt for attacks coming from without, but their bodies would not be oppressed with sickness, for God had delivered them from it. Had He not said, "If thou wilt diligently hearken to the voice of the Lord thy God . . . I will put none of these diseases upon thee which I have brought upon the Egyptians, for I am the Lord that healeth thee"? Again elsewhere, "Ye shall serve the Lord your God, . . . and I will take sickness away from the midst of thee" (Exod. 23:25; read also Lev. 26:14-16; Deut. 7:12-16; 28:15-61).

This calls our attention to a truth of the greatest importance: the intimate relations which exist between obedience and health, between sanctification which is the health of the soul, and the divine healing which ensures the health of the body—both are comprised in the salvation that comes from God. It is noteworthy that in several languages these three words, salvation, healing and sanctification, are derived from the same root and present the same fundamental thought. (For instance, the German *Heil,* salvation; *Heilung,* healing; *Heilichung,* sanctification.) Salvation is the redemption which the Savior has obtained for us; health is the salvation of the body which also comes to us from the Divine Healer; and lastly, sanctification reminds us that true salvation and true health consist in being holy as God is holy. Thus it is in giving health to the body and sanctification to the soul that Jesus is really the Savior of His people. Our text clearly declares the relation which exists between holiness of life and the healing of the body. The expressions which bear this out seem to be purposely multiplied: "If thou wilt diligently hearken . . . if thou wilt do that which is right . . . if thou wilt give ear . . . if thou wilt keep all his statutes, I will not send any sickness upon thee."

Here we have the key to all true obedience and holiness. We often think we know well the will of God revealed in His Word; but why does not this knowledge bring forth obedience? It is that in order to obey, we must begin by hearkening. "If thou wilt diligently hearken to the voice of the Lord thy God . . . and give ear. . . ." As long as the will of God reaches me through the voice of man, or through the reading of a book, it may have but little power with me, while if I enter into direct communion with God, and listen to His voice, His commandment is quickened with living power to facilitate its accomplishment.

Christ is the living Word, and the Holy Spirit is His voice. Listening to His voice means to renounce all our own will and wisdom, to close the ear to every other voice so as to expect no other direction but that of the Holy Spirit. One who is redeemed is like a servant or child who needs to be directed; he knows that he belongs entirely to God, and that all his being—spirit, soul, and body—ought to glorify God.

But he is equally conscious that this is above his strength, and that he needs to receive, hour by hour, the direction which he needs. He knows also that the divine commandment, as long as it is a dead letter to him, cannot impart to him strength and wisdom, and that it is only as he attentively gives ear that he will obtain the desired strength; therefore, he listens and learns thus to observe the laws of God. This life of attention and action, of renouncement and of crucifixion, constitutes a holy life. The Lord brings us to it in the first place by sickness, and makes us understand that which we are lacking, and then also by the healing which calls the soul to this life of continual attention to the voice of God.

Most Christians see nothing more in divine healing than a temporal blessing for the body, while in the promise of our holy God, its end is to make us holy. The call to holiness sounds daily stronger and more clearly in the Church. More and more believers are coming to understand that God wants them to be like Christ; and the Lord is beginning again to make use of His healing virtue, seeking thereby to show us that still in our own days, the Holy One of Israel is "The Lord that healeth thee," and that it is His will to keep His people both in health of body and in obedience.

Let him that looks for healing from the Lord receive it with joy. It is not a legal obedience which is required of him, an obedience depending upon his own strength. No, God asks of him, on the contrary, the abandonment of a little child, the attention which hearkens and consents to be led. This is what God expects of him; and the healing of the body will respond to this childlike faith, the Lord will reveal Himself to him as the mighty Savior who heals the body and sanctifies the soul.

Chapter 28

JOB'S SICKNESS AND HEALING

So went Satan forth from the presence of the Lord, and smote Job with sore boils, from the sole of his foot unto his crown. (Job 2:7)

The veil which hides from us the unseen world is lifted for a moment in the mysterious history of Job; it discovers to us heaven and hell occupied with God's servants upon earth. We see in it the temptations peculiar to sickness, and how Satan makes use of them to dispute with God, and to seek the perdition of the soul of man, while God, on the other hand, seeks to sanctify it by the very same trial. In the case of Job, we see in God's light whence proceeds sickness, what is the result which it should have, and how it is possible to be delivered from it.

Whence comes sickness—from God or from Satan? Opinions on this point vastly differ.

Some hold that it is sent of God, others see in it the work of the wicked one. Both are in error as long as they hold their view to the exclusion of that held by the other party, while both are in the right if they admit that there are two sides to this question. Let us say then that sickness comes from Satan, but that it cannot exist without the permission of God. On the other hand, the power of Satan is that of an oppressor, who has not himself any right to pounce upon man and attack him, and on the other hand, the claims of Satan on man are legitimate in that the righteousness of God decrees that he who yields himself to Satan places himself under his domination.

Satan is the prince of the kingdom of darkness and of sin; sickness is the consequence of sin. Herein is constituted the right of Satan over the body of sinful man. He is the prince of this world, so recognized by God, until such time as he shall be legally conquered and dethroned. Consequently, he has a certain power over all those who remain down here under his jurisdiction. He, then, it is who torments men with sickness, and seeks thereby to turn them from God, and to work their ruin.

But, we would haste to say, the power of Satan is far from being almighty; it can do nothing without God's authorization. God permits him to do all he does in tempting men, even believers, but it is in order that the trial may bring forth in them the fruit of holiness. It is also said that Satan has the power of death (Heb. 2:14), that he is everywhere at work where death reigns, but nevertheless, he has no power to decide as to the death of God's servants without the express will of God. It is even so with sickness. Because of sin, sickness is the work of Satan, but as the supreme direction of this world belongs to God, it can also be regarded as the work of God. All who are acquainted with the Book of Job know how very clearly this is brought out there.

What ought to be the result of sickness? The result will be good or evil according as God or Satan shall have the victory in us. Under Satan's influence, a sick person sinks always deeper in sin. He does not recognize sin to be the cause of the chastisement, and he occupies himself exclusively with himself and with his sufferings. He desires nothing but to be healed, without dreaming of a desire for deliverance from sin. But wherever God gains the victory, sickness leads the sufferer to renounce himself, and to abandon himself to God. The history of Job illustrates this.

His friends accused him, unjustly, of having committed sins of exceptional gravity, and by them to have drawn upon himself his terrible sufferings. It was, however, no such thing, since God Himself had borne him witness that he was "perfect and upright, one that feared God and eschewed evil" (Job 2:3). But in defending himself, Job went too far. Instead of humbling himself in abasement before the Lord, and recognizing his hidden sins, he sought in all self-righteousness to justify himself. It was not until the Lord appeared to him that he came to say, "I abhor myself, and repent in dust and ashes" (Job 42:6). To him, sickness became a signal blessing in bringing him to know God in quite a new way, and to humble himself more than ever before Him. This is the blessing which God desires that we also may receive whenever He permits Satan to strike us with sickness, and this end is attained by all sufferers who abandon themselves unreservedly to Him.

How are we to be delivered from sickness? A father never prolongs the chastisement of his child beyond the time necessary. God, also, who has His purpose in permitting sickness, will not prolong the chastisement longer than is needful to attain His end. As soon as Job had understood Him, from the time that he condemned himself and repented in dust and ashes, through hearkening to what God had revealed to him of Himself, the chastisement was at an end. God Himself delivered him from Satan's hand and healed him of his sickness.

Would that the sick in our day understood that God has a distinct purpose in permitting the chastisement, and that as soon as it is attained, as soon as the Holy Spirit shall have led them to confess and forsake their sins and to consecrate themselves entirely to the service of the Lord, the chastisement will no longer be needed—that the Lord could and would deliver them! God makes use of Satan as a wise government makes use of a jailer. He leaves His children in his power for the given time only, after which His good will is to associate us in the redemption of Him who has conquered Satan, who has withdrawn us from his domination in bearing in our stead our sins and our sicknesses.

Chapter 29

THE PRAYER OF FAITH

The prayer of faith shall save the sick, and the Lord shall raise him up. (James 5:15)

The prayer of faith! Only once does this expression occur in the Bible, and it relates to the healing of the sick. The Church has adopted this expression, but she hardly ever has recourse to the prayer of faith, but for the sake of obtaining other graces; while according to Scripture, it is especially intended for the healing of the sick.

Does the Apostle expect healing through the prayer of faith alone, or should it be accompanied by the use of remedies? This is generally the question which is raised. It is easily decided, if we take into consideration the power of the Church's spiritual life in the early ages; the gifts of healing bestowed on the Apostles by the Lord, augmented by the subsequent pouring out of the Holy Spirit (Acts 4:30; 5:15-16), what Paul says of "these gifts of healing by the same Spirit" (I Cor. 12:9), what James here insists upon when, in order to strengthen the reader in the expectation of faith, he recalls Elijah's prayer and God's wonderful answer (James 5:17-18). Does not all this clearly show that the believer is to look for healing in response to the prayer of faith alone, and without the addition of remedies?

Another question will arise: Does the use of remedies exclude the prayer of faith? To this, we believe our reply should be no, for the experience of a large number of believers testifies that in answer to their prayers God has often blessed the use of remedies, and made them a means of healing.

We come here to a third question: Which is then the line to follow that we may prove with the greatest certainty, and according to the will of God, the efficacy of the prayer of faith? Is it, according to James, in setting aside all remedies or in using remedies as believers do for the most part? In a word, is it with or without remedies that the prayer of faith best obtains the grace of God? Which of these two methods will be most directly to the glory of God and for blessing to the sick one?

Is it not perfectly simple to reply that if the prescription and the promise in James apply to believers of our time, they will find blessing in receiving them just as they were given to believers then, conforming to them on all points, expecting healing by the direct intervention of the Lord Himself, without having any recourse to remedies besides? It is, in fact, in this sense that Scripture always speaks of effectual faith and of the prayer of faith.

Both the laws of nature and the witness of Scripture show us that God often makes use of intermediary agencies to manifest His glory, but whether by experience or by Scripture, we know also that under the power of the fall, and the empire of our senses, our tendency is to attach more importance to the remedies than to the direct action of God. It often happens that remedies so occupy us as to intercept the presence of our God and turn us away from Him. Thus the laws and the properties of nature, which were destined to bring us back to God, have the contrary effect. This is why the Lord in calling Abraham to be the father of His chosen people had not recourse to the laws of nature (Rom. 4:17-21). God would form for Himself a people of faith, living more in the unseen than in the things visible; and in order to lead them into this life, it was necessary to take away their confidence in ordinary means. We see, therefore, that it was not by the ordinary ways which He has traced in nature that God led Abraham, Jacob, Moses, Joshua, Gideon, the Judges, David, and many other kings of Israel. His object was to teach them by this to confide only in Him, to know Him as He is: "Thou art the God that doest wonders" (Ps. 77:14).

God wills to act in a similar way with us. It is when we seek to walk according to His prescription in James 5, abandoning the things which are seen (II Cor. 4:18) to lay hold of the promise of God, and so receive directly from Him the desired healing, that we discover how much importance we have attached to earthly remedies. Doubtless there are Christians who can make use of remedies without damage to their spiritual life, but the larger number of them are apt to count much more on the remedies than on the power of God. Now the purpose of God is to lead His children into a more intimate communion with Christ, and this is just what does happen, when by faith we commit ourselves to Him as our sovereign Healer, counting solely on His invisible presence. Renouncing remedies strengthens faith in an extraordinary manner; healing becomes then far more than sickness, a source of numberless spiritual blessings; it makes real to us what faith can accomplish, it establishes a new tie between God and the believer, and commences in him a life of confidence and dependence. The body equally with the soul is placed under the power of the Holy Spirit, and the prayer of faith, which saves the sick, thus leads us to a life of faith, strengthened by the assurance that God manifests His presence in our earthly life.

Chapter 30

ANOINTING IN THE NAME OF THE LORD

Is any sick among you? Let him call for the elders of the church: and let them pray over him, anointing him with oil in the name of the Lord. (James 5:14)

James' instructions to anoint the sick person with oil in the name of the Lord have given rise to controversy. Some have sought to infer that, very far from prescribing recourse to the prayer of faith alone, without the use of remedies, Saint James had, on the contrary, mentioned anointing with oil as a remedy to be employed, and that to anoint in the name of the Lord had no other meaning than to rub the patient with oil. But as this prescription applies to all kinds of sickness, this would be to attribute to oil a miraculous virtue against all sickness. Let us see what the Scripture tells us about anointing with oil, and what sense it attaches to these two words.

It was the custom of the people in the East to anoint themselves with oil when they came out of the bath; it was most refreshing in a hot climate. We see also that all those who were called to the special service of God were to be anointed with oil, as a token of their consecration to God, and of the grace which they should receive from Him to fulfil their vocation. Thus the oil which was used to anoint the priests and the tabernacle was looked upon as "most holy" (Exod. 30:22-32), and wherever the Bible speaks of anointing with oil, it is an emblem of holiness and consecration. Nowhere in the Bible do we find any proof that oil was used as a remedy.

Anointing with oil is mentioned once in connection with sickness, but its place there was evidently as a religious ceremony and not as a remedy. In Mark 6:13, we read that the twelve "cast out many devils, and anointed with oil many that were sick, and healed them." Here the healing of the sick runs parallel with the casting out of devils: both the result of miraculous power. Such was the kind of mission which Jesus commanded His disciples when He sent them two and two: "He gave them power against unclean spirits, to cast them out, and to heal all manner of sickness and all manner of disease" (Matt. 10:1). Thus it was the same power which permitted them either to cast out devils or to heal the sick.

But let us seek to discover what was symbolized by the anointing administered by the twelve. In the Old Testament, oil was the symbol of the gift of the Holy Spirit: "The Spirit of the Lord God is upon me; because the Lord hath anointed me" (Isa. 61:1). It is said of the Lord Jesus in the New Testament, "God anointed Jesus of Nazareth with the Holy Ghost and with power" (Acts 10:38), and it is said of believers, "Ye have an unction [anointing, ASV] from the Holy One" (I John 2:20). Sometimes man feels the need of a visible sign, appealing to his senses, which may come to his aid to sustain his faith, and enable him to grasp the spiritual meaning. The anointing therefore should symbolize to the sick one the action of the Holy Spirit who gives the healing.

Do we then need the anointing as well as the prayer of faith? It is the Word of God which prescribes it, and it is in order to follow out its teachings that most of those who pray for healing receive the anointing; not that they regard it as indispensable, but to show that they are ready to submit to the Word of God in all things. In the last promise made by the Lord Jesus, He ordains the laying on of hands, not the anointing, to accompany the communication of healing virtue (Mark 16: 18). When Paul circumcised Timothy and took upon himself a special vow, it was to prove that he had no objection to observe the institutions of the Old Covenant as long as the liberty of the Gospel did not thereby suffer loss. In the same way, James, the head of the Church of Jerusalem, faithful in preserving as far as possible the institutions of his fathers, continued the system of the Holy Spirit. And we also should regard it, not as a remedy, but as a pledge of the mighty virtue of the Holy Spirit, as a means of strengthening faith, a point of contact and of communion between the sick one and the members of the Church who are called to anoint him with oil.

"I am the Lord that healeth thee" (Exod. 15:26).

Chapter 31

FULL SALVATION OUR HIGH PRIVILEGE

Son, thou art ever with me, and all that I have is thine. (Luke 15:31)

We may talk a great deal, and write a great deal, about the father's love to the prodigal, but when we think of the way he treated the elder brother, it brings to our hearts a truer sense of the wonderful love of the father.

I suppose there are not a few readers of this book who have got "full salvation"; but perhaps more than half of you have not got it, and, if I were to ask you, "Have you got it?" you would probably say, "I don't understand what you mean by it; what is it?" Well, the great object of this book is to bring you to see that full salvation is waiting for you now, that God wants you to experience it, and, if you feel you have not got it, we wish to show you how wrong it is to be without it, and then to show you how to come out of the wrong life into the right one here and now. Oh, may all who have not got the experience pray very humbly, "Oh, my Father, bring me into the full enjoyment of Thy full salvation."

First, then, the elder son, being ever with his father, had, if he liked, the privilege of two things: unceasing fellowship and unlimited partnership. But he was worse than the prodigal, for, although always at home, yet he had never known, nor enjoyed, nor understood the privileges that were his. All this fullness of fellowship had been waiting for and offered to him, but he had not received it. While the prodigal was away from home in the far country, his elder brother was far from the enjoyment of home, while he was at home.

Full salvation includes unceasing fellowship: "Ever with me." An earthly father loves his child, and delights to make his child happy. "God is love," and He delights to pour out His own nature on His people. Many people talk about God hiding His face, but there are only two things that ever caused God to do so—sin or unbelief. Nothing else can. It is the very nature of the sun to shine, and it can't help shining on and on. "God is love," and, speaking with all reverence, He can't help loving. We see His goodness toward the ungodly, and His compassion on the erring, but His fatherly love is manifested toward all His children. But, you say, "Is it possible to be always happy and dwelling with God?" Yes, certainly, and there are many Scripture promises as to this. Look at the Epistle to the Hebrews, where we read of "boldness to enter within the veil"; how often, too, does David speak of hiding "in the secret of his tabernacle," and "dwelling under the shadow of the almighty."

My message is that the Lord your God desires to have you living continually in the light of His countenance. Your business, your temper, your circumstances, of which you complain as hindering, are they stronger than God? If you come and ask God to shine in and upon you, you will see and prove that He can do it, and that you as a believer may walk all the day and every day in the light of His love. That is "full salvation."

"Ever with Thee"; I never knew it, Lord, and so I did not enjoy it, but I do now.

Full salvation includes unlimited partnership: "All I have is thine." The elder son complained of the father's gracious reception of the prodigal, of all the feasting and rejoicing over his return, while he had never been given a kid that he might make merry with his friends. The father, in the tenderness of his love, answers him, "Son, you were always in my house; you had only to ask and you would have got all you desired and required." And that is what our Father says to all His children. But you are saying, "I am so weak, I cannot conquer my sins; I can't manage to keep right; I can't do this and the other thing." No, but God can; and all the time He is saying to you, "All I have is thine; for in Christ I have given it to you. All the Spirit's power and wisdom, all the riches of Christ, all the love of the Father; there is nothing that I have but is thine; I as God am God, that I may love, keep, and bless thee." Thus God speaks, but it seems all a dream to some. Why are you so poor? God's Word is sure, and does He not promise all this? See in John, chapters 14 to 16, how He tells us that we may have wonderful answers to prayer if we come in Jesus' name and abide in Him. Do we really believe that it is possible for a Christian to live such a life?

Now, we have looked at this high privilege which is for all, so we pass on to consider the low experience of many of God's dear children. What is it? Just living in poverty and starvation. The elder son, the child of a rich man, living in utter poverty!—"never had a kid," while all that was his father's was his—just exactly the state of many a child of God. The way He wants us to live is in the fullest fellowship of all His blessings, yet what a contrast!

Ask some if their lives are full of joy; why, they don't even believe it is possible to be always happy and holy. "How could we get on thus in business?" they say; and they imagine that the life of fullest blessing possible to them must be one of sighing and sadness and sorrow.

I asked a dear devoted Christian woman how she was getting on. She answered that in her experience it was sometimes light and sometimes darkness, and argued that, as this was so in nature, the same thing held good in the kingdom of grace. So she just gave herself up to a wretched experience. But I don't read in the Bible that there is to be any night or darkness in the believer's experience; on the contrary, I read, "Thy sun shall no more go down"; (Isa. 60:20) yet there are many who actually believe that there is nothing so good for them. Again, nothing can hide God from us but sin and unbelief. If you are in spiritual poverty, and there is no joy, no experience of victory over sin, temper, wandering, why is it so? "Oh," you say, "I'm too weak, I must fall." But does not the Scripture say that He is "able to keep you from falling (stumbling)"? A minister once told me that, although God is able, the verse does not say He is willing to do it. God does not mock us, beloved. If He says He is "able," then it is a proof of His willingness to do it. Do let us believe God's Word and examine our own experience in the light of it.

Again, are you working and bearing much fruit for God, and do people by your life see and say, "God is with that man, keeping him humble, pure, and heavenly minded"? Or are they forced to confess that you are just a very ordinary Christian, easily provoked, worldly, and not heavenly minded? That is not the life God wants us to live, brethren. We have a rich Father, and as no true earthly father would like to see his child in rags, or without shoes and proper clothing, etc., neither does our God; but He wishes to fill up our life with richest and choicest blessings.

How many Sunday school teachers there are who teach, and teach, and hope for the conversion of their scholars, but yet they can't say God uses them in the conversion of any of them. They enjoy no close fellowship with God, no victory over sin, no power to convince the world. To which class do you belong? The low-level, or the fully possessed? Confess it today. These two sons represent two classes of Christians: the prodigal—away backslidden; the elder son—out of full fellowship with God; they were alike poor, and the elder son needed as great a change as did the prodigal; he needed to repent and confess and claim his full privileges; and so ought all low-level Christians to repent, confess, and claim full salvation. Both of you, come today and say, "Father, I have sinned."

Now, we ask, What is the cause of this terrible discrepancy? Why the great difference in the experience, I wonder? Ask yourself, "What is the reason I am not enjoying this full blessing? God's Word speaks of it, others speak of it, and I see some who are living in it." Oh, do ask the reason. Come to God and say, "Why is it I never live the life You want me to live?"

You will find the answer in our story. The elder son had an unchildlike spirit, and entertained wrong thoughts about his father; and, if you had known the real character of your Father, your life would have been all right. You have, as it were, said, "I never got a kid to make merry; my Father is rich, but He never gives. I have prayed quite enough, but

God does not answer me. I hear other people say that God fills and satisfies them, but He never does that for me."

A dear minister told me once that an abundant life was not for everybody, that it was of God's sovereignty to give this to whomsoever He pleased. Friends, there is no doubt as to God's sovereignty. He dispenses His gifts as He will. We are not all Pauls or Peters; places at the right and left hand of God are prepared for whomsoever He will. But this is not a matter of divine sovereignty, it is a question of child's heritage. The Father's love offers to give to every child in actual experience His full salvation. Now look at an earthly father. His children are of various ages, but all have equal right to the joy of their father's countenance. True, he gives to his son of twenty years more money than to the son of five, and he has more to speak of to the boy of fifteen than to the child of three; but, as regards his love toward them, it is all the same, and in their privileges as children, they are all alike. And God's love to His dear children is all the same. Oh, do not try to throw the blame on God, but say, "I have had hard thoughts of Thee, O God, and I have sinned. As a father, I have done for my children what I did not believe God was able and willing to do for me, and I have been lacking in child-like faith." Oh, do believe in the love, the willingness and power of God to give you full salvation, and a change must surely come.

Now let us consider the way of restoration, how to get out of this poor experience. The prodigal repented, and so must those children of God who have been living within sight of, but not enjoying His promises. Conversion is generally sudden, and a long repentance is usually a long impenitence. Many in the Church of Christ think it must take a long time to get into full salvation. Yes, it will take a long time if you are to do it yourself—indeed, you never will. No, no, friend, if you come and trust God, it can be done in a moment. By God's grace give yourself up to Him. Don't say, "What's the use? it will do no good"; but put yourself, as you are in sin and weakness, into the bosom of your Father. God will deliver you, and you will find that it is only one step out of the darkness into the light. Say, "Father, what a wretch I have been, in being with Thee and yet not believing Thy love to me!"

Yes, I come today with a call to "repent," addressed, not to the unsaved, but to those who know what it is to be pardoned. For have you not sinned in the hard thoughts you have had of God, and is there not a longing, a thirsting and hungering after something better? Come, then, repent, and just believe that God does blot out the sin of your unbelief. Do you believe it? Oh, do not dishonor God by unbelief, but come today and confidently claim full salvation. Then trust in Him to keep you. This seems difficult to some, but there is no difficulty about it. God will shine His light upon you always, saying, "Son, thou art ever with me"; and all you have to do is to dwell in and walk in that light.

I began by saying there are two classes of Christians: those who enjoy full salvation, and those who do not understand about it. Well, if it is not clear to you, ask God to make it clear. But if you do understand about it, remember it is a definite act. Just let yourself go into the arms of God. Hear Him say, "All is thine"; then you say, "Praise God, I believe, I accept, I give up myself to Him, and I believe God gives Himself now to me!"

Chapter 32

YE ARE THE BRANCHES

Ye are the branches. (John 15:5)

What a simple thing it is to be a branch, the branch of a tree, or the branch of a vine! The branch grows out of the vine, or out of the tree, and there it lives and in due time bears fruit. It has no responsibility except just to receive from the root and stem sap and nourishment. And if we only by the Holy Spirit knew our relationship to Jesus Christ, our work would be changed into the brightest and most heavenly thing upon earth. Instead of there ever being soul-weariness or exhaustion, our work would be like a new experience, linking us to Jesus as nothing else can. Is it not often true that our work comes between us and Jesus? What folly! The very work He has to do in me, and I for Him, I take up in such a way that it separates me from Christ. Many a laborer in the vineyard has complained that he has too much work, and not time for close communion with Jesus, and that his usual work weakens his inclination for prayer, and that his too much intercourse with men darkens the spiritual life. Sad thought, that the bearing of fruit should separate the branch from the vine! That must be because we have looked upon our work as something else than the branch bearing fruit. May God deliver us from every false thought about the Christian life.

Now, just a few thoughts about this blessed branch-life.

In the first place, it is a life of absolute dependence. The branch has nothing: it depends upon the vine for everything. That word, absolute dependence, is one of the most solemn and large and precious of words. A great German theologian wrote two large volumes some years ago, to show that the whole of Calvin's theology is summed up in that one principle of absolute dependence upon God; and he was right. If you can learn every moment of the day to depend upon God, everything will come right. You will get the higher life if you depend absolutely upon God.

Must I understand that when I have got to

work, when I have to preach a sermon, or address a Bible class, or to go out and visit the poor neglected ones, that all the responsibility of the work is on Christ?

That is exactly what Christ wants you to understand. Christ wants that in all your work, the very foundation should be the simple, blessed consciousness: Christ must care for all.

And how does He fulfill the trust of that dependence? He does it by sending down the Holy Spirit—not now and then only as a special gift, for remember the relation between the vine and the branches is such that hourly, daily, unceasingly, there is the living connection maintained. The sap does not flow for a time, and then stop, and then flow again, but from moment to moment the sap flows from the vine to the branches. And just so, my Lord Jesus wants me to take that blessed position as a worker, and, morning by morning and day by day and hour by hour and step by step, in every work I have to go out to, just to abide before Him in the simple, utter helplessness of one who knows nothing, and is nothing, and can do nothing.

Absolute dependence upon God is the secret of all power in work. The branch has nothing but what it gets from the vine, and you and I can have nothing but what we get from Jesus.

Secondly, the life of the branch is not only a life of entire dependence, but of deep restfulness. Oh, that little branch, if it could think, and if it could feel, and if it could speak—and if we could have a little branch today to talk to us, and if we would say, "Come, branch of the vine, tell me, I want to learn from you how I can be a true branch of the living Vine," what would it answer? The little branch would whisper, "Man, I hear that you are wise, and I know that you can do a great many wonderful things. I know you have much strength and wisdom given to you, but I have one lesson for you. With all your hurry and effort in Christ's work, you never prosper. The first thing you need is to come and rest in your Lord Jesus. That is what I do. Since I grew out of that vine, I have spent years and years, and all I have done is just to rest in the vine. When the time of spring came, I had no anxious thought nor care. The vine began to pour its sap into me, and to give the bud and leaf. And when the time of summer came, I had no care, and in the great heat, I trusted the vine to bring moisture to keep me fresh. And in the time of harvest, when the owner came to pluck the grapes, I had no care. If there was anything in the grapes not good, the owner never blamed the branch; the blame was always on the vine. And if you would be a true branch of Christ, the living Vine, just rest on Him. Let Christ bear the responsibility."

You say, "Won't that make me slothful?" I tell you it will not. No one who learns to rest upon the living Christ can become slothful, for the closer your contact with Christ, the more of the Spirit of His zeal and love will be borne in upon you. A man sometimes tries and tries to be dependent upon Christ, but he worries himself about this absolute dependence: he tries and he cannot get it. But let him sink down into entire restfulness every day.

Rest in Christ, who can give wisdom and strength, and you do not know how that restfulness will often prove to be the very best part of your message. You plead with people and you argue, and they get the idea: There is a man arguing and striving with me. They only feel: Here are two men dealing with each other. But if you will let the deep rest of God come over you, the rest in Christ Jesus, the peace and rest and holiness of heaven, that restfulness will bring a blessing to the heart, even more than the words you speak.

But a third thought. The branch teaches a lesson of much fruitfulness. You know the Lord Jesus repeated that word fruit often in that parable; He spoke first of fruit, and then of more fruit, and then of much fruit. Yes, you are ordained not only to bear fruit, but to bear much fruit. "Herein is My Father glorified, that ye bear much fruit." In the first place, Christ said, "I am the Vine, and My Father is the Husbandman who has charge of Me and you." He who will watch over the connection between Christ and the branches is God; and it is in the power of God, through Christ, we are to bear fruit.

O Christians! you know this world is perishing for the want of workers. And it wants not only more workers. The workers are saying, some more earnestly than others, "We need not only more workers, but we need our workers to have a new power, a different life—that the workers should be able to bring more blessing."

What is wanting? There is wanting the close connection between the worker and the heavenly Vine. Christ, the heavenly Vine, has blessings that He could pour on tens of thousands who are perishing. Christ, the heavenly Vine, has power to provide the heavenly grapes. But "ye are the branches," and you cannot bear heavenly fruit unless you are in close connection with Jesus Christ.

Do not confound work and fruit. There may be a good deal of work for Christ that is not the fruit of the heavenly Vine. Do not seek for work only. Study this question of fruit-bearing. It means the very life and the very power and the very Spirit and the very love within the heart of the Son of God—it means the heavenly Vine Himself coming into your heart and mine.

Stand in close connection with the heavenly Vine and say: "Lord Jesus, nothing less than the sap that flows through Thyself, nothing less than the Spirit of Thy divine life is what we ask. Lord Jesus, I pray Thee let Thy Spirit flow through me in all my work for Thee." I tell you again that the sap of the heavenly Vine is nothing but the Holy Spirit. The Holy Spirit is nothing but the life of the heavenly Vine, and what you must get from Christ is nothing less than a strong inflow of the Holy Spirit. You need it exceedingly, and you want nothing more than that. Remember that. Do not expect Christ to give a bit of strength here, and a bit of blessing yonder, and a bit of help over there. As the vine does its work in giving its own peculiar sap to the branch, so expect Christ to give His own Holy Spirit into your heart, and then you will bear much fruit. And if you have only begun to bear fruit, and are listening to the word of Christ in the parable, "more fruit," "much fruit," remember that in order that you should bear more fruit, you just require more of Jesus in your life and heart.

A fourth thought. The life of the branch is a life of close communion. Let us again ask: What has the branch to do? You know that precious inexhaustible word that Christ used: Abide. Your life is to be an abiding life. And how is the abiding to be? It is to be just like the branch in the vine, abiding every minute of the day. There are the branches, in close communion, in unbroken communion, with the vine, from January to December. And cannot I live every day—it is to me an almost terrible thing that we should ask the question—cannot I live in abiding communion with the heavenly Vine? You say, "But I am so much occupied with other things." You may have ten hours' hard work daily, during which your brain has to be occupied with temporal things; God orders it so. But the abiding work is the work of the heart, not of the brain, the work of the heart clinging to and resting in Jesus, a work in which the Holy Spirit links us to Christ Jesus. Oh, do believe that deeper down than the brain, deep down in the inner life, you can abide in Christ, so that every moment you are free the consciousness will come: Blessed Jesus, I am still in Thee. If you will learn for a time to put aside other work and to get into this abiding contact with the heavenly Vine, you will find that fruit will come.

What is the application to our life with regard to this abiding communion? What does it mean? It means close fellowship with Christ in secret prayer. I am sure there are Christians who do long for the higher life, and who sometimes have got a great blessing, and have at times found a great inflow of heavenly joy and a great outflow of heavenly gladness; and yet after a time, it has passed away. They have not understood that close, personal actual communion with Christ is an absolute necessity for daily life. Take time to be alone with Christ. Nothing in heaven or earth can free you from the necessity for that, if you are to be happy and holy Christians.

Oh, how many Christians look upon it as a burden, and a tax, and a duty, and a difficulty to get much alone with God! That is the great hindrance to our Christian life everywhere. We need more quiet fellowship with God, and I tell you in the name of the heavenly

Vine that you cannot be healthy branches, branches into which the heavenly sap can flow, unless you take plenty of time for communion with God. If you are not willing to sacrifice time to get alone with Him, and give Him time every day to work in you, and to keep up the link of connection between you and Himself, He cannot give you that blessing of His unbroken fellowship. Jesus Christ asks you to live in close communion with Him. Let every heart say, "O Christ, it is this I long for, it is this I choose." And He will gladly give it to you.

And then my last thought. The life of the branch is a life of entire surrender. This word, "entire surrender," is a great and solemn word, and I believe we do not understand its meaning. But yet the little branch preaches it. "Have you anything to do, little branch, beside bearing grapes?" "No, nothing." "Are you fit for nothing?" "Fit for nothing!" The Bible says that a bit of vine cannot even be used as a pen; it is fit for nothing but to be burned. "And now, what do you understand, little branch, about your relation to the vine?" "My relation is just this: I am utterly given up to the vine, and the vine can give me as much or as little sap as it chooses. Here I am at its disposal, and the vine can do with me what it likes."

Oh, we need this entire surrender to the Lord Jesus Christ. This is one of the most difficult points to make clear, and one of the most important and needful points to explain—what this entire surrender is. It is an easy thing for a man or a number of men to offer themselves up to God for entire consecration, and to say, "Lord it is my desire to give up myself entirely to Thee." That is of great value, and often brings very rich blessing. But the one question I ought to study quietly is: What is meant by entire surrender? It means that just as literally as Christ was given up entirely to God, I am given up entirely to Christ. Is that too strong? Some of you think so. Some think that never can be; that just as entirely and absolutely as Christ gave up His life to do nothing but seek the Father's pleasure, and depend on the Father absolutely and entirely, I am to do nothing but to seek the pleasure of Christ. But that is actually true. Christ Jesus came to breathe His own Spirit into us, to make us find our very highest happiness in living entirely for God, just as He did. O beloved brethren, if that is the case, then I ought to say, "Yes, as true as it is of that little branch of the vine, so true, by God's grace, I would have it be of me. I would live day by day that Christ may be able to do with me what He will."

Ah! here comes the terrible mistake that lies at the bottom of so much of our own religion. A man thinks, "I have my business and family duties, and my relations as a citizen, and all this I cannot change. And now alongside of all this, I am to take in religion and the service of God as something that will keep me from sin. God help me to perform my duties properly!"

That is not right. When Christ came, He came and bought the sinner with His blood. If there were a slave market here and I were to buy a slave, I should take that slave away to my own house from his old surroundings, and he would live at my house as my personal property, and I could order him about all the day. And if he were a faithful slave, he would live as having no will and no interests of his own, his one care being to promote the well-being and honor of his master. And in like manner I, who have been bought with the blood of Christ, have been bought to live every day with the one thought—How can I please my Master?

Oh, we find the Christian life so difficult because we seek for God's blessing while we live in our own will. We should be glad to live the Christian life according to our own liking. We make our own plans and choose our own work, and then we ask the Lord Jesus to come in and take care that sin shall not conquer us too much, and that we shall not go too far wrong; we ask Him to come in and give us so much of His blessing. But our relation to Jesus ought to be such that we are entirely at His disposal, and every day come to Him humbly and straightforwardly, and say: Lord, is there anything in me that is not according to Thy will, that has not been ordered by Thee, or that is not entirely given up to Thee? Oh, if we would wait and wait patiently, there would spring up a relationship between us and Christ so close and so tender, that we should afterward be amazed how far distant our intercourse with Him had previously been.

I know there are a great many difficulties about this question of holiness; I know that all do not think exactly the same with regard to it. But that would be to me a matter of comparative indifference if I could see that all are honestly longing to be free from every sin. But I am afraid that unconsciously there are in hearts often compromises with the idea: We cannot be without sin; we must sin a little every day—we cannot help it. Oh, that people would actually cry to God: "Lord, do keep me from sin!" Give yourself utterly to

Jesus, and ask Him to do His very utmost for you in keeping you from sin.

In conclusion, let me gather up all in one word. Christ Jesus said, "I am the vine, ye are the branches." In other words: I, the living One who have so completely given Myself to you, am the Vine. You cannot trust Me too much. I am the Almighty Worker, full of a divine life and power. Christians, you are the branches of the Lord Jesus Christ. If there is in your heart the consciousness: I am not a strong, healthy, fruit-bearing branch, I am not closely linked with Jesus, I am not living in Him as I should be—then listen to Him saying, "I am the Vine, I will receive you, I will draw you to Myself, I will bless you, I will strengthen you, I will fill you with My Spirit. I, the Vine, have taken you to be My branches; I have given Myself utterly to you; children, give yourselves utterly to Me. I have surrendered Myself as God absolutely to you; I became Man and died for you that I might be entirely yours. Come and surrender yourselves entirely to be Mine."

What shall our answer be? Oh, let it be a prayer from the depths of our heart, that the living Christ may take each one of us and link us close to Himself. Let our prayer be that He, the living Vine, shall so link each of us to

Himself that we shall go on our way with our hearts singing: He is my Vine, and I am His branch; I want nothing more—now I have the everlasting Vine. Then when you get alone with Him, worship and adore Him, praise and trust Him, love Him and wait for His love. Thou art my Vine, and I am Thy branch. It is enough, my soul is satisfied. Glory to His blessed name!